Great-Tasting Recipes with SPAM® Luncheon Meat

Publications International, Ltd.

Favorite All Time Recipes is a trademark of Publications International, Ltd., 7373 N. Cicero Ave., Lincolnwood, IL 60646.

Photography: Sanders Studio, Inc., Chicago

Photography on pages 13, 31, 37, 39, 53, 63, 73, 87 and 91 by Tad Ware & Company, Inc., Minneapolis, MN.

Pictured on the front cover *(clockwise from top right):* Marinated SPAM™ Vegetable Salad *(page 36)*, Spicy SPAM™ Party Dip *(page 10)* and SPAM™ Vegetable Strudle *(page 92)*.

Pictured on the back cover *(top to bottom)*: SPAMBURGER® Hamburger *(page 40)*, SPAM™ Pinwheels *(page 8)* and SPAM™ Pasta & Spinach Salad *(page 34)*.

ISBN: 0-7853-1402-4

Manufactured in U.S.A.

8   7   6   5   4   3   2   1

Nutritional Analysis: Nutritional information is given for the recipes in this publication. Each analysis is based on the food items in the ingredient list, except ingredients labeled as "optional" or "for garnish." When more than one ingredient choice is listed, the first ingredient is used for analysis. If a range for the amount of ingredient is given, the nutritional analysis is based on the lowest amount. Foods offered as "serve with" suggestions are not included in the analysis unless otherwise stated.

Contents

The SPAM® Luncheon Meat Story

There are very few products that are as popular and highly recognized as SPAM® Luncheon Meat. An all-American favorite in the familiar blue and yellow can, SPAM® has long been the top-selling canned luncheon meat in America.

SPAM® Luncheon Meat was introduced in 1937, but it was during World War II that SPAM® first rose to fame. Since SPAM® required absolutely no refrigeration to keep it fresh and great tasting, it quickly became a military staple. Following World War II, Hormel Foods combined America's newfound patriotism with a SPAM® Luncheon Meat promotion that enlisted the help of The Hormel Girls. This 60-member performing troupe traveled throughout the country in the late 1940s and early 1950s singing popular show tunes and providing samples of SPAM® Luncheon Meat in supermarkets and through door-to-door appearances. In 1940 Hormel Foods introduced what is said to have been the first singing commercial. Featuring George Burns and Gracie Allen backed by Artie Shaw and his 23-piece orchestra, this ad sent SPAM® sales skyrocketing.

Much of SPAM®'s success through the years is attributed to meeting the ever-changing needs and lifestyles of consumers. Various sizes and varieties of SPAM® Luncheon Meat have been developed to offer consumers choices to suit their preferences. The Original SPAM® Luncheon Meat, sold in a 12-ounce can, stood alone until 1962 when the 7-ounce can size was introduced to appeal to smaller families and single-person households. In 1971, smoke-flavor SPAM® Luncheon Meat became available, soon to be followed by SPAM® Less Sodium Luncheon Meat. In 1992, SPAM® Lite Luncheon Meat, containing 50% less fat than Original SPAM® Luncheon Meat, hit supermarket shelves. The most recent addition to the SPAM® Luncheon Meat family came in early 1995, with the introduction of the 7-ounce can of SPAM® Lite Luncheon Meat. Since its debut back in 1937, more than five billion cans of SPAM® have been sold worldwide.

While SPAM® remains as popular as ever all across America, it is king in Austin, Minnesota. Austin is home for the Hormel Foods Corporation—a multinational processor of well-known meat and food products and the town's largest employer. With this in mind, it is easy to see why the people of Minnesota love their SPAM®. Austin has earned a title that no other city in America can claim—SPAM™TOWN USA. One of the largest events held there annually is the SPAM™ Jam celebration. This celebration takes place every July and includes a variety of contests and activities ranging from art and recipe contests to the "Hog Jog 5-mile run," bike races and games. There is also plenty of entertainment on hand to add to the festivities. This local event provides patrons an opportunity to sample fabulous recipes such as SPAMBLED™ Egg Muffins and SPAMBURGER® Hamburgers.

After more than 50 years in the marketplace, SPAM® Luncheon Meat continues to be an American favorite. Breeze through this outstanding collection of creative recipes featuring SPAM® Luncheon Meat and see for yourself why everyone loves the great taste of SPAM®!

Snacks & Appetizers

SPAM™ Pinwheels

1 (1-pound) loaf frozen bread dough, thawed
¼ cup pizza sauce
1 (7-ounce) can SPAM® Luncheon Meat,
   cubed
2 cups (8 ounces) shredded mozzarella cheese
2 tablespoons chopped pepperoncini
Additional pizza sauce

Roll bread dough out onto lightly floured surface to 12-inch square. Brush pizza sauce over bread dough. Sprinkle SPAM®, cheese and pepperoncini over dough. Roll dough, jelly-roll fashion; pinch seam to seal (do not seal ends). Cut roll into 16 slices. Place slices, cut side down, on greased baking sheet. Cover and let rise in warm place 45 minutes. Heat oven to 350°F. Bake 20 to 25 minutes or until golden brown. Serve immediately with additional pizza sauce.   *Makes 16 appetizer servings*

NUTRITIONAL INFORMATION PER SERVING:
Calories 146; Protein 8 g; Carbohydrates 15 g; Fat 6 g; Cholesterol 19 mg; Sodium 619 mg

Spicy SPAM™ Party Dip

2 (8-ounce) packages cream cheese, softened
1 (12-ounce) can SPAM® Luncheon Meat
2 tablespoons Worcestershire sauce
1 teaspoon CHI-CHI'S® Salsa Dash cayenne pepper
1 cup finely chopped green or red bell peppers
½ cup chopped celery
¼ cup chopped onion
2 tablespoons chopped fresh cilantro Crackers, chips and/or vegetables

In medium bowl, combine cream cheese, SPAM®, Worcestershire sauce, salsa and cayenne pepper. Beat at medium speed of electric mixer until smooth. Stir in bell pepper, celery, onion and cilantro. Cover and refrigerate 1 hour. Serve with crackers, chips and vegetables.

Makes 4 cups dip

NUTRITIONAL INFORMATION PER SERVING:
Calories 36; Protein 1 g; Carbohydrates 0.5 g;
Fat 3 g; Cholesterol 12 mg; Sodium 79 mg

SPAM™ Cantina Appetizers

1 (12-ounce) can SPAM® Luncheon Meat, cubed
1 tomato, chopped
1 avocado, peeled and chopped
½ cup chopped celery
½ cup chopped green onions
½ cup CHI-CHI'S® Picante Sauce
3 tablespoons chopped fresh parsley
1 tablespoon lemon juice
1 tablespoon peanut oil
1 teaspoon garlic salt
12 (8-inch) flour tortillas

In large skillet over medium-high heat, sauté SPAM® until lightly browned. In medium bowl, combine SPAM®, tomato, avocado, celery and green onions. In small bowl, stir together picante sauce, parsley, lemon juice, peanut oil and garlic salt. Add picante sauce mixture to skillet; toss with SPAM™ mixture. Serve with tortillas. *Makes 12 appetizer servings*

NUTRITIONAL INFORMATION PER SERVING:
Calories 206; Protein 8 g; Carbohydrates 22 g;
Fat 11 g; Cholesterol 23 mg; Sodium 431 mg

Spicy SPAM™ Party Dip

Easy SPAM™ Triangles

1 (7-ounce) can SPAM® Luncheon Meat, cut into small cubes
¾ cup (3 ounces) shredded Gouda cheese
½ cup diced, peeled apple
2 tablespoons onion sour cream dip
1 (15-ounce) package refrigerated pie crusts
1 egg white, beaten
Nonstick cooking spray
¼ teaspoon poppy seeds

Heat oven to 425°F. In medium bowl, combine SPAM®, cheese, apple and dip. Cut one pie crust sheet into 8 wedges. Place ¼ cup SPAM™ mixture in center of each wedge, spreading to within ½ inch of each edge. Moisten edges of pastry with egg white. Cut remaining pie crust sheet into 8 wedges. Place over filling. Press edges of filled pastry firmly together using fork. Place on baking sheet coated with nonstick cooking spray. Brush with remaining egg white and sprinkle with poppy seeds. Bake 15 to 20 minutes or until lightly browned.

Makes 8 servings

NUTRITIONAL INFORMATION PER SERVING:
Calories 324; Protein 16 g; Carbohydrates 19 g;
Fat 22 g; Cholesterol 46 mg; Sodium 798 mg

Speedy SPAM™ Dip

1 (12-ounce) can SPAM® Luncheon Meat
1 onion
2 jalapeño peppers, seeded
4 tablespoons mayonnaise or salad dressing
Chips and/or crackers

In food processor fitted with metal blade, process SPAM®, onion and jalapeño peppers until smooth. Stir in mayonnaise. Cover and refrigerate 1 hour. Serve with chips and crackers.   *Makes 2 cups dip*

NUTRITIONAL INFORMATION PER SERVING:
Calories 34; Protein 2 g; Carbohydrates 0.3 g;
Fat 3 g; Cholesterol 9 mg; Sodium 130 mg

Top to bottom: Easy SPAM™
Triangles; Speedy SPAM™ Dip

SPAM™ Fiesta Dip

**1 (15-ounce) can CHI-CHI'S®
Refried Beans
1 (1¼-ounce) package taco seasoning
½ cup chopped green onions
1 (12-ounce) can SPAM® Luncheon
Meat, cubed
1 (15-ounce) can HORMEL® Chili
No Beans
1 cup (4 ounces) shredded Cheddar
cheese
1 cup (4 ounces) shredded Monterey
Jack cheese
1 cup sour cream
Sliced ripe olives
CHI-CHI'S® Salsa
CHI-CHI'S® Tortilla Chips**

Heat oven to 350°F. In small bowl,
combine refried beans and taco seasoning.
Spread mixture onto bottom of 12-inch
pizza pan. Layer green onions, SPAM®,
chili and cheeses in pan. Bake 20 to 25
minutes or until hot and cheese is melted.
Spread sour cream over top. Sprinkle with
olives. Serve with salsa and tortilla chips.
Makes about 24 appetizer servings

NUTRITIONAL INFORMATION PER SERVING:
Calories 129; Protein 7 g; Carbohydrates 24 g;
Fat 8 g; Cholesterol 28 mg; Sodium 432 mg

Broiled SPAM™ Appetizers

**1 (7-ounce) can SPAM® Luncheon
Meat, finely cubed
⅓ cup shredded Cheddar cheese
¼ cup finely chopped celery
¼ cup mayonnaise or salad dressing
1 tablespoon chopped fresh parsley
⅛ teaspoon hot pepper sauce
Toast triangles, party rye slices or
crackers**

In medium bowl, combine all ingredients
except toast. Spread mixture on toast
triangles. Place on baking sheet. Broil 1
to 2 minutes or until cheese is melted.
Makes 32 appetizers

NUTRITIONAL INFORMATION PER SERVING:
Calories 20; Protein 1 g; Carbohydrates 0 g;
Fat 2 g; Cholesterol 6 mg; Sodium 72 mg

SPAM™ Quesadillas

1 (12-ounce) can SPAM® Luncheon Meat, chopped
4 cups (16 ounces) shredded Monterey Jack cheese with peppers
6 (8-inch) flour tortillas, divided
Guacamole and CHI-CHI'S® Salsa

In large bowl, combine SPAM® and cheese. Spoon SPAM™ mixture over each of 3 tortillas. Top with remaining 3 tortillas. On lightly greased griddle over medium-high heat, heat 1 quesadilla until soft and cheese is melted, turning once. Repeat with remaining 2 quesadillas. Cut each tortilla stack into 6 wedges. Serve with guacamole and salsa.

Makes 18 appetizer servings

NUTRITIONAL INFORMATION PER SERVING:
Calories 166; Protein 10 g; Carbohydrates 7 g;
Fat 11 g; Cholesterol 37 mg; Sodium 366 mg

Mini SPAM® & Cheese Buns

1 (1-pound) loaf frozen bread dough, thawed
1 (12-ounce) can SPAM® Luncheon Meat, shredded
1½ cups (6 ounces) shredded Monterey Jack cheese
2 teaspoons dried dill weed
1 egg
1 tablespoon water

Cut bread dough in half lengthwise; cut each half into 12 pieces. In medium bowl, combine SPAM®, cheese and dill weed; mix well. Place about 1 tablespoon SPAM™ mixture in center of 1 piece of dough. Shape dough into a ball; place on greased baking sheet. Repeat with remaining dough pieces. Cover; let rise in warm place 30 to 40 minutes or until doubled in bulk. Heat oven to 350°F. Uncover dough. In small bowl, stir together egg and water. Brush each piece of dough with egg mixture. Bake 20 to 30 minutes or until golden brown. Serve warm.* *Makes 24 appetizers*

* To reheat buns, wrap in aluminum foil. Bake 10 to 15 minutes or until thoroughly heated. Buns can be frozen. Seal in freezer-weight plastic food storage bags and freeze up to 2 months. Reheat as directed.

NUTRITIONAL INFORMATION PER SERVING:
Calories 108; Protein 6 g; Carbohydrates 10 g;
Fat 5 g; Cholesterol 27 mg; Sodium 276 mg

SPAM™ Cheese Torte

1 cup finely crushed butter crackers
¼ cup butter or margarine, melted
1 tablespoon water
1 (12-ounce) can SPAM® Luncheon Meat, shredded
2 cups (8 ounces) shredded Cheddar cheese
1 (3-ounce) package cream cheese, softened
2 tablespoons finely chopped onion
1 teaspoon prepared horseradish
1 teaspoon Worcestershire sauce
½ teaspoon dry mustard
½ teaspoon chili powder
½ cup chopped pecans
Assorted crackers

Heat oven to 350°F. In small bowl, combine crushed crackers, butter and water; press firmly onto bottom of greased 9-inch springform pan. Bake 10 minutes. Cool. In large bowl, beat together SPAM®, Cheddar cheese, cream cheese, onion, horseradish, Worcestershire sauce, dry mustard and chili powder. Spread over crust. Cover. Refrigerate overnight. To serve, press nuts over top. Remove side of pan; place torte on serving tray. Cut circle about 2 inches from outer edge of torte. Cut entire torte into 16 wedges. Cut outer circle wedges in half. Serve with crackers.

Makes 48 appetizer servings

NUTRITIONAL INFORMATION PER SERVING:
Calories 62; Protein 3 g; Carbohydrates 1 g; Fat 5 g; Cholesterol 15 mg; Sodium 116 mg

SPAM™ Nachos

1 (10½-ounce) bag CHI-CHI'S® Tortilla Chips
1 (12-ounce) can SPAM® Luncheon Meat, cubed
1 (16-ounce) jar CHI-CHI'S® Salsa
1 (15-ounce) can CHI-CHI'S® Refried Beans
1 (8-ounce) package shredded Mexican pasteurized processed cheese

Heat oven to 425°F. Place chips on baking sheet. Sprinkle SPAM® over chips. In medium bowl, combine salsa and refried beans; pour over chips. Sprinkle with cheese. Bake 6 to 7 minutes or until cheese is melted. Serve immediately.

Makes 10 appetizer servings

NUTRITIONAL INFORMATION PER SERVING:
Calories 361; Protein 16 g; Carbohydrates 28 g; Fat 21 g; Cholesterol 48 mg; Sodium 1034 mg

SPAM™ Nachos

Salads, Soups & Stews

SPAM™ Tostada Salad

8 (7-inch) flour tortillas
1 tablespoon vegetable oil
1 (12-ounce) can SPAM® Luncheon Meat, cut
    into ½-inch strips
1 onion, cut into wedges
4 cups torn romaine lettuce
2 tomatoes, chopped
1 (2¼-ounce) can sliced ripe olives, drained
1 cup (4 ounces) shredded Monterey Jack
    cheese
    CHI-CHI'S® Salsa

In large skillet over medium-high heat, cook tortillas in hot oil 2 to 3 minutes or until crisp; set aside. In same skillet, cook SPAM® and onion 7 to 10 minutes or until SPAM® is browned. Meanwhile, toss together lettuce, tomatoes, olives and cheese. Place SPAM™ mixture on top of tortillas. Top with lettuce mixture. Serve with salsa.

Makes 4 servings

NUTRITIONAL INFORMATION PER SERVING:
Calories 553; Protein 28 g; Carbohydrates 47 g; Fat 30 g; Cholesterol 93 mg; Sodium 1310 mg

SPAM™ Vegetable Soup with Cheese-Topped Croutons

1½ cups chopped carrots
1 cup chopped onion
1 tablespoon vegetable oil
5 cups chicken broth
3 cups chopped cabbage
1 cup diced, unpeeled potatoes
½ teaspoon dried thyme leaves
1 (12-ounce) can SPAM® Luncheon
   Meat, cubed

Cheese-Topped Croutons

1¼ cups (5 ounces) shredded Swiss
   cheese
⅓ cup mayonnaise or salad dressing
2 tablespoons grated Parmesan cheese
2 tablespoons sliced green onion
6 slices sourdough bread, toasted

In 3- or 4-quart saucepan over medium heat, sauté carrots and chopped onion in oil 5 to 10 minutes or until onion is golden. Stir in broth, cabbage, potatoes and thyme. Bring to a boil. Cover. Reduce heat and simmer 30 minutes or until vegetables are tender. Stir in SPAM®. Simmer 2 minutes.

Meanwhile, heat broiler. In small bowl, combine Swiss cheese, mayonnaise, Parmesan cheese and green onion. Spread over each bread slice. Ladle soup into oven-proof bowls.* Top each with a bread

slice. Place bowls on baking sheet. Broil 3 minutes or until cheese mixture just begins to brown.   *Makes 6 servings*

* If bowls are not ovenproof, place bread slices on baking sheet and broil, then place on top of soup.

NUTRITIONAL INFORMATION PER SERVING:
Calories 470; Protein 25 g; Carbohydrates 29 g;
Fat 29 g; Cholesterol 76 mg; Sodium 1576 mg

Three Bean SPAM™ Salad

1 (16-ounce) can cut green beans,
   drained
1 (16-ounce) can kidney beans,
   drained
1 (16-ounce) can yellow wax beans,
   drained
1 (7-ounce) can SPAM® Luncheon
   Meat, cubed
⅓ cup chopped onion
⅓ cup sugar
⅓ cup vegetable oil
⅓ cup cider vinegar
1 tablespoon stone-ground mustard
¼ teaspoon coarsely ground black
   pepper

In large bowl, combine green beans, kidney beans, wax beans, SPAM® and onion. In small bowl, combine remaining ingredients; pour over SPAM™ mixture. Stir gently. Cover and refrigerate several hours or overnight.   *Makes 10 servings*

NUTRITIONAL INFORMATION PER SERVING:
Calories 215; Protein 9 g; Carbohydrates 19 g;
Fat 12 g; Cholesterol 27 mg; Sodium 738 mg

*SPAM™ Vegetable Soup with
Cheese-Topped Croutons*

Singapore SPAM™ Salad

Warm Sesame Dressing

1 cup sugar
$^1\!/_3$ cup rice vinegar
$^1\!/_4$ cup olive oil
2 tablespoons sesame oil
$^1\!/_4$ teaspoon garlic salt

Salad

$^1\!/_2$ head iceberg lettuce, thinly sliced
$^1\!/_2$ head romaine lettuce, thinly sliced
1 (12-ounce) can SPAM® Luncheon
Meat, cubed
3 carrots, grated
1 cup chopped green onions
1 cup chopped celery
1 green bell pepper, chopped
1 cup thinly sliced radishes
1 (6$^1\!/_2$-ounce) package sliced almonds,
toasted

In small saucepan over low heat, combine all dressing ingredients. Stir constantly until sugar dissolves. In large bowl, toss together all salad ingredients. Serve warm dressing with salad.   *Makes 8 servings*

NUTRITIONAL INFORMATION PER SERVING:
Calories 432; Protein 13 g; Carbohydrates 36 g;
Fat 28 g; Cholesterol 34 mg; Sodium 453 mg

SPAM® & Potato Chowder

2 tablespoons butter or margarine
$^1\!/_3$ cup shredded carrot
$^1\!/_4$ cup finely chopped onion
4 cups milk
3 cups peeled, diced potatoes
2 (10$^3\!/_4$-ounce) cans cream of chicken
soup
1 (12-ounce) can SPAM® Luncheon
Meat, cubed
$^1\!/_2$ teaspoon dried thyme leaves

In 4-quart saucepan, melt butter. Stir in carrot and onion. Cook, stirring occasionally, until onion is tender. Stir in remaining ingredients; mix well. Cook over medium-high heat, stirring occasionally, until mixture comes to a boil. Reduce heat to medium. Cover. Cook, stirring occasionally, until potatoes are tender.   *Makes 6 servings*

NUTRITIONAL INFORMATION PER SERVING:
Calories 420; Protein 19 g; Carbohydrates 39 g;
Fat 21 g; Cholesterol 76 mg; Sodium 1466 mg

Singapore SPAM™ Salad

SPAM™ Western Pasta Salad

3 cups cooked macaroni
1 (12-ounce) can SPAM® Luncheon Meat, cubed
1 cup (4 ounces) cubed Cheddar cheese
1 cup shredded carrots
¾ cup chopped celery
¼ cup chopped green bell pepper
¼ cup chopped onion
½ cup mayonnaise or salad dressing
2 tablespoons creamy mustard blend
1½ tablespoons barbecue sauce

In large bowl, combine macaroni, SPAM®, cheese, carrots, celery, bell pepper and onion. In small bowl, combine remaining ingredients; toss with macaroni mixture. Cover; refrigerate 1 hour. *Makes 8 servings*

NUTRITIONAL INFORMATION PER SERVING:
Calories 328; Protein 13 g; Carbohydrates 19 g; Fat 22 g; Cholesterol 57 mg; Sodium 674 mg

SPAM™ Broccoli Rice Soup

1 (4.5-ounce) package broccoli rice au gratin
2 cups water
1 tablespoon butter or margarine
2 cups milk
1 (10¾-ounce) can cream of broccoli soup
1 (7-ounce) can SPAM® Luncheon Meat, diced
¼ cup (1 ounce) shredded Cheddar cheese

In large saucepan, combine broccoli rice au gratin, water and butter. Heat to boiling. Cover and simmer 20 minutes. Add milk, soup, SPAM® and cheese. Heat to boiling, stirring occasionally.
Makes 6 to 8 servings

NUTRITIONAL INFORMATION PER SERVING:
Calories 264; Protein 13 g; Carbohydrates 22 g; Fat 14 g; Cholesterol 48 mg; Sodium 1034 mg

SPAM™ Skillet Potato Salad

1 (12-ounce) can SPAM® Luncheon Meat, cut into strips
½ cup chopped green onions
½ cup chopped green bell pepper
3 medium potatoes, boiled and diced
1½ cups (6 ounces) shredded sharp Cheddar cheese
¼ cup mayonnaise or salad dressing

In large skillet over medium heat, sauté SPAM®, green onions and bell pepper until SPAM® is lightly browned. Add potatoes, cheese and mayonnaise. Heat just until cheese begins to melt.
Makes 6 servings

NUTRITIONAL INFORMATION PER SERVING:
Calories 353; Protein 18 g; Carbohydrates 15 g; Fat 25 g; Cholesterol 80 mg; Sodium 792 mg

SPAM® and Peanut Salad

Dressing

⅓ cup rice wine vinegar
¼ cup olive oil
2 tablespoons peanut butter
1 tablespoon HOUSE OF TSANG®
   Light Soy Sauce
1 teaspoon sugar
¼ teaspoon ground ginger
1 garlic clove, minced

Salad

2 cups shredded napa cabbage or
   lettuce
2 cups shredded romaine lettuce
1 (12-ounce) can SPAM® Luncheon
   Meat, cut into 2-inch strips
1 cup shredded carrots
1 cup fresh or thawed frozen pea pods
½ cup roasted peanuts
¼ cup chopped green onions

In small bowl, using wire whisk or fork, whisk together all dressing ingredients. In large bowl, combine all salad ingredients. Drizzle with dressing.

Makes 6 servings

NUTRITIONAL INFORMATION PER SERVING:
Calories 326; Protein 15 g; Carbohydrates 11 g;
Fat 26 g; Cholesterol 46 mg; Sodium 676 mg

SPAM™ Broccoli Pecan Salad

1 (12-ounce) can SPAM® Luncheon
   Meat, cut into strips
¾ pound broccoli, broken into florets,
   blanched
¼ pound Cheddar cheese, cut into
   matchstick-size pieces
½ cup thinly sliced radishes
¼ cup white wine vinegar
3 tablespoons olive oil
2 tablespoons sugar
1 garlic clove, minced
½ teaspoon dry mustard
¼ cup toasted pecans

In large skillet over medium heat, sauté SPAM® until lightly browned. In large bowl, combine SPAM®, broccoli, cheese and radishes. In small bowl, combine vinegar, oil, sugar, garlic and dry mustard. Toss dressing with SPAM™ mixture. Cover and refrigerate 1 hour. Before serving, stir in toasted pecans.

Makes 6 servings

NUTRITIONAL INFORMATION PER SERVING:
Calories 317; Protein 16 g; Carbohydrates 10 g;
Fat 24 g; Cholesterol 65 mg; Sodium 700 mg

Ragin' Cajun SPAM™ Party Salad

Salad

8 ounces uncooked wagon wheel
    shape pasta
1 (6-ounce) jar marinated artichoke
    hearts
1 (12-ounce) can SPAM® Luncheon
    Meat, cubed
1 cup diced green bell peppers
½ cup chopped red onion
½ cup sliced ripe olives
3 tablespoons finely chopped fresh
    basil

Dressing

⅓ cup olive oil
¼ cup creole seasoning mix
1 tablespoon lemon juice
1 tablespoon mayonnaise or salad
    dressing
1 tablespoon white wine vinegar
½ teaspoon dry mustard
½ teaspoon dried oregano leaves
½ teaspoon sugar
½ teaspoon dried thyme leaves
1 clove garlic, chopped

Cook pasta according to package
directions. Drain artichokes, reserving
marinade; cut into quarters. In large bowl,
combine all salad ingredients. In blender,
combine reserved artichoke marinade
with dressing ingredients; process until
smooth. Add dressing to salad, tossing
well. Cover and refrigerate several hours
or overnight.   *Makes 8 to 10 servings*

NUTRITIONAL INFORMATION PER SERVING:
Calories 325; Protein 11 g; Carbohydrates 26 g;
Fat 20 g; Cholesterol 35 mg; Sodium 669 mg

Scrumptious SPAM™ Spring Chili

Nonstick cooking spray
4 cloves garlic, minced
2 green bell peppers, cut into strips
1 cup sliced green onions
3 (4.25-ounce) jars CHI-CHI'S®
    Diced Green Chilies
2 jalapeño peppers, seeded and
    minced
2 teaspoons dried oregano leaves
2 teaspoons ground cumin
2 (15-ounce) cans cannellini beans or
    kidney beans
2 (10¾-ounce) cans condensed
    chicken broth, undiluted
1 (12-ounce) can SPAM® Luncheon
    Meat, cubed

In large saucepan coated with cooking
spray, sauté garlic over medium heat 1
minute. Add bell peppers, green onions,
chilies, jalapeños, oregano and cumin;
sauté 5 minutes. Stir in beans and broth.
Bring to a boil. Cover. Reduce heat and
simmer 10 minutes. Stir in SPAM®.
Simmer 2 minutes.

Makes 4 to 6 servings

NUTRITIONAL INFORMATION PER SERVING:
Calories 437; Protein 33 g; Carbohydrates 45 g;
Fat 15 g; Cholesterol 69 mg; Sodium 3582 mg

Scrumptious SPAM™ Spring Chili

SPAM™ Stew with Buttermilk Topping

1 (10¾-ounce) can cream of chicken soup
½ cup milk
½ cup chopped onion
1 (3-ounce) package cream cheese, cubed
¼ cup shredded carrot
¼ cup chopped celery
¼ cup (1 ounce) grated Parmesan cheese
1 (12-ounce) can SPAM® Luncheon Meat, cubed
1 (10-ounce) package frozen cut broccoli, cooked and drained
1 cup buttermilk pancake mix
1 cup (4 ounces) shredded Cheddar cheese
¼ cup milk
1 egg, beaten
1 tablespoon vegetable oil
¼ cup sliced almonds

Heat oven to 375°F. In large saucepan, combine soup, ½ cup milk, onion, cream cheese, carrot, celery and Parmesan cheese. Cook and stir until cream cheese is melted. Stir in SPAM® and broccoli; heat thoroughly. Pour into 2-quart casserole. In medium bowl, combine pancake mix and Cheddar cheese. In small bowl, stir together ¼ cup milk, egg and oil. Add to pancake mix; stir until combined. Spoon topping over SPAM™ mixture. Sprinkle with almonds. Bake 20 to 25 minutes or until topping is golden brown. *Makes 6 to 8 servings*

NUTRITIONAL INFORMATION PER SERVING:
Calories 472; Protein 24 g; Carbohydrates 28 g;
Fat 30 g; Cholesterol 125 mg; Sodium 1561 mg

SPAM™ Italian Rice Salad

2 cups uncooked long-grain white rice
9 green onions, chopped
1½ teaspoons paprika
½ teaspoon ground cumin
¼ cup olive oil
2 (14½-ounce) cans chicken broth
1 (12-ounce) can SPAM® Luncheon Meat, cut into strips
1 (10-ounce) package frozen peas, thawed and drained
1 green bell pepper, cut into ¼-inch strips
1 red bell pepper, cut into ¼-inch strips
1 (3½-ounce) package HORMEL® Sliced Pepperoni
½ cup chopped fresh parsley

In 3-quart saucepan over medium heat, cook rice, green onions, paprika and cumin in oil until onions are tender. Stir in broth. Cook over low heat 20 to 30 minutes or until rice is tender and all liquid is absorbed. Meanwhile, in large skillet over medium heat, sauté SPAM® 4 to 5 minutes. Combine rice mixture, SPAM®, peas, bell peppers, pepperoni and parsley. *Makes 10 servings*

NUTRITIONAL INFORMATION PER SERVING:
Calories 342; Protein 14 g; Carbohydrates 36 g;
Fat 15 g; Cholesterol 35 mg; Sodium 836 mg

SPAM™ Italian Rice Salad

SPAM™ Corn Chowder

1 cup chopped onion
1 tablespoon butter or margarine
1½ cups diced, peeled potatoes
½ cup chopped green bell pepper
2 (17-ounce) cans cream-style corn
2 cups milk
1 (12-ounce) can SPAM® Luncheon Meat, cubed

In 3-quart saucepan over medium heat, sauté onion in butter 5 to 10 minutes or until golden. Add potatoes and bell pepper. Cook and stir 2 minutes. Add corn and milk. Bring to a boil. Reduce heat and simmer 15 minutes or until potatoes are tender, stirring occasionally. Stir in SPAM®. Simmer 2 minutes.

Makes 6 to 8 servings

NUTRITIONAL INFORMATION PER SERVING:
Calories 366; Protein 17 g; Carbohydrates 52 g;
Fat 12 g; Cholesterol 56 mg; Sodium 1242 mg

SPAM™ Western Bean Soup

1 cup chopped onion
1 tablespoon vegetable oil
3 (10½-ounce) cans condensed chicken broth
1 (14½-ounce) can tomatoes, cut up
1 cup sliced carrots
⅓ cup chili sauce
3 tablespoons packed brown sugar
3 tablespoons cider vinegar
2 teaspoons Worcestershire sauce
2 teaspoons prepared mustard
2 (15½-ounce) cans pinto beans, rinsed and drained
1 (12-ounce) can SPAM® Luncheon Meat, cubed
2 tablespoons chopped fresh parsley

In 5-quart saucepan, sauté onion in oil until golden. Stir in chicken broth, tomatoes, carrots, chili sauce, brown sugar, vinegar, Worcestershire sauce and mustard. Mash half the beans with fork; add mashed beans and whole beans to soup. Blend well. Bring to a boil. Cover. Reduce heat and simmer 30 minutes or until carrots are tender. Stir in SPAM® and parsley. Simmer 2 minutes.

Makes 6 servings

NUTRITIONAL INFORMATION PER SERVING:
Calories 331; Protein 22 g; Carbohydrates 34 g;
Fat 13 g; Cholesterol 46 mg; Sodium 2263 mg

*Top to bottom: SPAM™ Corn Chowder;
SPAM™ Western Bean Soup*

Zesty SPAM™ Caesar Salad

½ cup prepared Caesar salad dressing
1 (12-ounce) can SPAM® Luncheon
  Meat, cut into 2-inch strips
1 garlic clove, crushed
6 cups torn romaine lettuce
½ cup (2 ounces) grated Parmesan
  cheese
  Seasoned bread cubes

In large skillet, heat dressing. Stir in
SPAM® and garlic. Cook, stirring
occasionally, until thoroughly heated.
Place lettuce in large bowl. Spoon
SPAM™ mixture over lettuce; toss gently.
Top with Parmesan cheese and bread
cubes.   *Makes 6 servings*

NUTRITIONAL INFORMATION PER SERVING:
Calories 218; Protein 14 g; Carbohydrates 2 g;
Fat 17 g; Cholesterol 67 mg; Sodium 832 mg

SPAM™ Salad Cones

1 (12-ounce) can SPAM® Luncheon
  Meat, cubed
1 cup chopped celery
½ cup chopped green bell pepper
⅓ cup mayonnaise or salad dressing
¼ cup toasted slivered almonds
2 tablespoons chopped onion
2 tablespoons pickle relish
1 teaspoon prepared mustard
5 (8-inch) flour tortillas
5 lettuce leaves

In medium bowl, combine all ingredients
except tortillas and lettuce. Cover;
refrigerate until ready to serve. Roll each
tortilla into large cone and secure with
wooden picks. Carefully stuff each cone
with crumpled piece of foil so cone will
retain shape. Place cones on baking sheet.
Broil, 3 inches from heat source, turning
several times until cones are crisp and
lightly browned, about 3 minutes. Cool;
carefully remove foil and wooden picks.
When ready to serve, line each cone with
lettuce leaf and fill with salad mixture.
                          Makes 5 servings

NUTRITIONAL INFORMATION PER SERVING:
Calories 440; Protein 15 g; Carbohydrates 25 g;
Fat 28 g; Cholesterol 63 mg; Sodium 968 mg

Classic SPAM™ Potato Salad

2 pounds (about 6 medium) potatoes
1 (12-ounce) can SPAM® Luncheon Meat, cubed
½ cup cooked diced carrots
½ cup frozen peas, thawed
½ cup chopped dill pickles
¼ cup finely chopped onion
¾ cup mayonnaise or salad dressing
2 tablespoons dill pickle liquid
1 teaspoon prepared mustard

Cook unpeeled potatoes in boiling water until tender; drain. Cool slightly; peel. Cool to room temperature; cut into ½-inch cubes. In large bowl, combine potatoes and SPAM®. Add carrots, peas, pickles and onion; gently toss. Stir together mayonnaise, pickle liquid and mustard; gently stir into SPAM™ mixture. Cover and refrigerate several hours.

Makes 8 to 10 servings

NUTRITIONAL INFORMATION PER SERVING:
Calories 344; Protein 10 g; Carbohydrates 26 g;
Fat 23 g; Cholesterol 46 mg; Sodium 672 mg

Vineyard SPAM™ Salad

1 (12-ounce) can SPAM® Luncheon Meat, cubed
⅔ cup mayonnaise or salad dressing
1 tablespoon lime juice
1 teaspoon dry mustard
2 cups seedless grapes
1 cup pea pods, cut in half
½ cup thinly sliced red onion

In large skillet over high heat, sauté SPAM® 2 minutes, stirring constantly; set aside. In small bowl, combine mayonnaise, lime juice and dry mustard. In large bowl, combine SPAM®, grapes, pea pods and onion. Toss with mayonnaise mixture. Cover and refrigerate 1 hour. *Makes 6 servings*

NUTRITIONAL INFORMATION PER SERVING:
Calories 336; Protein 10 g; Carbohydrates 13 g;
Fat 28 g; Cholesterol 59 mg; Sodium 700 mg

SPAM™, Pasta & Spinach Salad

Dressing

¹/₃ cup thawed frozen orange juice
    concentrate
¹/₄ cup plain yogurt
 1 tablespoon olive oil
 1 teaspoon packed brown sugar
¹/₈ teaspoon ground nutmeg
¹/₈ teaspoon black pepper

Salad

6 ounces uncooked bow tie pasta or
    elbow macaroni
6 cups torn fresh spinach
1 (12-ounce) can SPAM® Luncheon
    Meat, cut into 2-inch strips
1 cup sliced celery
1 orange, peeled, sectioned, sections
    cut in half
¹/₂ cup thinly sliced red onion rings

In small bowl using wire whisk or fork, whisk together all dressing ingredients; set aside. Cook pasta according to package directions; drain. In large bowl, combine all salad ingredients; toss gently. Pour dressing over salad; toss gently. Serve immediately.　　*Makes 6 servings*

NUTRITIONAL INFORMATION PER SERVING:
Calories 299; Protein 16 g; Carbohydrates 35 g;
Fat 11 g; Cholesterol 45 mg; Sodium 632 mg

SPAM™ Mexican Extravaganza

1 cup uncooked tri-color rotini
1 (12-ounce) can SPAM® Luncheon
    Meat, cubed
1 (15-ounce) can pinto beans, drained
1 cup frozen whole kernel corn,
    thawed
³/₄ cup (3 ounces) shredded Cheddar
    cheese
1 green bell pepper, chopped
¹/₄ cup chopped onion
¹/₄ cup chopped tomato
1 (2¹/₄-ounce) can sliced ripe olives,
    drained
1 (8-ounce) jar CHI-CHI'S® Salsa
³/₄ cup sour cream
1 tablespoon mayonnaise or salad
    dressing
4 cups shredded lettuce
    CHI-CHI'S® Tortilla Chips

Cook rotini according to package directions; drain and refrigerate. In large skillet over medium heat, sauté SPAM® until lightly browned; cool. In large bowl, combine rotini, SPAM®, beans, corn, cheese, bell pepper, onion, tomato and olives. In small bowl, combine salsa, sour cream and mayonnaise. Toss together salsa mixture and SPAM™ mixture. Cover and refrigerate several hours. Spoon salad mixture over lettuce. Serve with chips.
　　Makes 6 to 8 servings

NUTRITIONAL INFORMATION PER SERVING:
Calories 403; Protein 20 g; Carbohydrates 31 g;
Fat 23 g; Cholesterol 86 mg; Sodium 1053 mg

SPAM™, Pasta &
Spinach Salad

■ ■ ■ ■ ■ ■ ■ ■ ■ ■ ■ ■ ■ ■ ■ ■ ■ ■ ■ ■

Marinated SPAM™ Vegetable Salad

1 (12-ounce) can SPAM® Luncheon
   Meat, cut into strips
1 pound broccoli, broken into florets
1 head cauliflower, broken into florets
2 cups cooked rotini
1 cup sliced mushrooms
1 cup chopped celery
1 onion, chopped
½ cup chopped red bell pepper
1½ cups olive oil
1 cup sugar
½ cup vinegar
¼ cup chopped fresh parsley
2 teaspoons dry mustard

In large skillet over medium heat, sauté SPAM® until lightly browned. In large bowl, combine SPAM®, broccoli, cauliflower, rotini, mushrooms, celery, onion and bell pepper. In small bowl, combine oil, sugar, vinegar, parsley and dry mustard; mix well. Toss dressing with SPAM™ mixture. Cover and refrigerate 4 hours or overnight.   *Makes 12 servings*

NUTRITIONAL INFORMATION PER SERVING:
Calories 422; Protein 8 g; Carbohydrates 30 g;
Fat 31 g; Cholesterol 23 mg; Sodium 338 mg

SPAM™ Golden Rice Salad

1 (12-ounce) can SPAM® Luncheon
   Meat, cut into strips
2 cups cooked wild rice, brown rice or
   white rice
1 yellow bell pepper, chopped
½ cup chopped carrot
½ cup coarsely chopped pecans,
   toasted
½ cup golden raisins
   Sherry Chive Vinaigrette (recipe
   follows)
   Lettuce cups (optional)

In large bowl, combine all ingredients except lettuce cups. Cover and refrigerate 4 hours or overnight. Serve in lettuce cups, if desired.   *Makes 6 servings*

Sherry Chive Vinaigrette

In blender container, combine ⅓ cup olive oil, 2 tablespoons sherry wine vinegar, ¼ cup snipped fresh chives, 1 tablespoon chopped fresh parsley, 1 clove garlic and ¼ teaspoon freshly ground black pepper. Cover and process until chives are minced.

NUTRITIONAL INFORMATION PER SERVING:
Calories 394; Protein 13 g; Carbohydrates 30 g;
Fat 26 g; Cholesterol 45 mg; Sodium 577 mg

Top to bottom: Marinated SPAM™ Vegetable Salad; SPAM™ Golden Rice Salad

Sensational Sandwiches

Dipped SPAM™ Swiss Sandwiches

1 (12-ounce) can SPAM® Luncheon Meat, cut
    into 12 slices
6 (1-ounce) slices Swiss cheese
12 slices white bread
3 eggs
6 tablespoons milk
3 tablespoons butter or margarine
    Soft-spread strawberry cream cheese

Layer SPAM® and Swiss cheese on each of 6 bread slices; top with remaining 6 bread slices. In shallow bowl, beat together eggs and milk. Dip both sides of each sandwich in egg mixture. In large skillet or griddle over medium heat, cook sandwiches in butter until cheese melts and sides are golden brown. Serve with strawberry cream cheese.

Makes 6 servings

NUTRITIONAL INFORMATION PER SERVING:
Calories 465; Protein 26 g; Carbohydrates 31 g; Fat 26 g; Cholesterol 195 mg; Sodium 1017 mg

SPAMBURGER® Hamburgers

1 (12-ounce) can SPAM® Luncheon
    Meat
6 hamburger buns, split
3 tablespoons mayonnaise
6 lettuce leaves
2 tomatoes, sliced
6 (1-ounce) slices American cheese

Slice SPAM® into 6 slices (3×¼-inch). In large skillet, sauté SPAM® until lightly browned. Spread mayonnaise on buns. Layer remaining ingredients on bun bottoms. Cover with bun tops.

Makes 6 servings

NUTRITIONAL INFORMATION PER SERVING:
Calories 405; Protein 20 g; Carbohydrates 25 g;
Fat 25 g; Cholesterol 76 mg; Sodium 1280 mg

SPAMBLED™ Denver Sandwiches

1 (12-ounce) can SPAM® Luncheon
    Meat, chopped
¼ cup finely chopped onion
1 tablespoon vegetable oil
4 eggs, beaten
8 slices bread, toasted

In small skillet, cook and stir SPAM® and onion in oil until onion is tender. Pour eggs into skillet. Cook over low heat just until set. Cut into four wedges; turn. Cook until light brown. Serve each wedge between two bread slices.

Makes 4 servings

NUTRITIONAL INFORMATION PER SERVING:
Calories 424; Protein 25 g; Carbohydrates 30 g;
Fat 22 g; Cholesterol 281 mg; Sodium 1188 mg

Grilled Garden SPAM™ Salad Sandwiches

1 (12-ounce) can SPAM® Luncheon
    Meat, finely cubed
1 cup (4 ounces) shredded Swiss
    cheese, divided
½ cup thinly sliced celery
½ cup chopped green bell pepper
⅓ cup mayonnaise or salad dressing
½ teaspoon dried thyme leaves
12 slices caraway rye bread
¼ cup butter or margarine, softened
1 tomato, thinly sliced
1 small onion, thinly sliced, separated
    into rings

In medium bowl, combine SPAM®, ½ cup Swiss cheese, celery, bell pepper, mayonnaise and thyme; mix well. Spread each bread slice on one side with butter. Spread ½ cup SPAM™ mixture on unbuttered side of each of 6 bread slices. Top each with tomato slices, onion rings and about 1 tablespoon of the remaining ½ cup Swiss cheese. Top with remaining bread slices, buttered side up. In large skillet or griddle over medium heat, cook sandwiches until cheese melts and sides are golden brown. *Makes 6 servings*

NUTRITIONAL INFORMATION PER SERVING:
Calories 470; Protein 20 g; Carbohydrates 30 g;
Fat 31 g; Cholesterol 91 mg; Sodium 1046 mg

SPAMBURGER® Hamburger

SPAM™ French Bread Pizza

1 onion, chopped
1 green bell pepper, chopped
1 cup sliced fresh mushrooms
1 tablespoon vegetable oil
1 (16-ounce) loaf French bread
1 (12-ounce) can SPAM® Luncheon Meat, cubed
1 cup chunky-style spaghetti sauce
2 cups (8 ounces) shredded mozzarella cheese

Heat oven to 425°F. In large skillet, sauté vegetables in oil 3 to 4 minutes or until tender. Cut bread in half lengthwise. Remove soft center, leaving two bread shells. Spoon vegetables and SPAM® into bread shells. Spoon spaghetti sauce over SPAM®. Sprinkle with cheese. Place shells on baking sheet. Bake 10 to 15 minutes or until cheese is melted and bubbly. *Makes 8 servings*

NUTRITIONAL INFORMATION PER SERVING:
Calories 373; Protein 20 g; Carbohydrates 39 g; Fat 15 g; Cholesterol 52 mg; Sodium 1005 mg

Broiled SPAM® & Spinach Sandwiches

½ cup mayonnaise or salad dressing
¼ cup country-style Dijon mustard
1 teaspoon prepared horseradish
6 slices sourdough bread
1 (12-ounce) can SPAM® Luncheon Meat, cut into 12 slices
1 (9-ounce) package frozen chopped spinach, thawed and drained
6 thin slices red onion, separated into rings
2 cups (8 ounces) shredded mozzarella cheese

In small bowl, combine mayonnaise, mustard and horseradish; mix well. Spread 1 to 2 tablespoons mayonnaise mixture on one side of each bread slice. Top each with 2 slices SPAM®, and ⅙ of the spinach, onion rings and cheese. Place on broiler pan. Broil 4 to 6 inches from heat source 2 to 3 minutes or until cheese is melted and sandwich is thoroughly heated. *Makes 6 servings*

NUTRITIONAL INFORMATION PER SERVING:
Calories 454; Protein 23 g; Carbohydrates 22 g; Fat 31 g; Cholesterol 79 mg; Sodium 1172 mg

SPAM™ French Bread Pizza

SPAM™ Veggie Pita Pockets

1 (7-ounce) can SPAM® Luncheon Meat, cubed
1 cup chopped broccoli
1 cup chopped cauliflower
1 tomato, chopped
1 carrot, peeled and chopped
⅓ cup chopped cucumber
⅓ cup finely chopped onion
½ cup Italian salad dressing
4 pita pocket breads, cut in half

In large bowl, combine SPAM®, broccoli, cauliflower, tomato, carrot, cucumber and onion. Toss with dressing. Cover and refrigerate several hours. Spoon salad mixture into pocket bread.

Makes 8 servings

NUTRITIONAL INFORMATION PER SERVING:
Calories 216; Protein 8 g; Carbohydrates 22 g;
Fat 11 g; Cholesterol 20 mg; Sodium 539 mg

SPAM™ Imperial Tortilla Sandwiches

1 (12-ounce) can SPAM® Luncheon Meat, cubed
1 (8-ounce) package cream cheese, softened
⅓ cup chopped green onions
2 tablespoons chopped fresh dill
3 (8-inch) flour tortillas
1 medium cucumber, peeled and thinly sliced
½ cup alfalfa sprouts
¼ cup sunflower seeds

In medium bowl, combine SPAM® and cream cheese. Stir in green onions and dill. Spread ⅓ of SPAM™ mixture evenly over each tortilla. Top with ⅓ each cucumber, alfalfa sprouts and sunflower seeds. Roll up tortilla jelly-roll fashion and wrap in plastic wrap. Repeat with remaining tortillas. Refrigerate 2 hours. To serve, cut each roll in half.

Makes 6 servings

NUTRITIONAL INFORMATION PER SERVING:
Calories 338; Protein 15 g; Carbohydrates 14 g;
Fat 25 g; Cholesterol 87 mg; Sodium 741 mg

SPAM™ Veggie Pita Pocket

California SPAMBURGER® Hamburgers

1 (12-ounce) can SPAM® Luncheon Meat
6 whole wheat hamburger buns, split
3 tablespoons Thousand Island salad dressing
6 lettuce leaves
2 tomatoes, sliced
6 green bell pepper rings
6 onion slices

Slice SPAM® into 6 slices (3×¼-inch). In large skillet over medium heat, sauté SPAM® until lightly browned. Spread cut sides of buns with dressing. Layer lettuce, SPAM®, tomatoes, bell pepper and onion on bun bottoms. Cover with bun tops.
Makes 6 servings

NUTRITIONAL INFORMATION PER SERVING:
Calories 287; Protein 14 g; Carbohydrates 28 g;
Fat 13 g; Cholesterol 47 mg; Sodium 891 mg

SPAM™ Grilled Cheese Hero

4 (1-ounce) slices Swiss cheese
2 plum tomatoes, thinly sliced
8 slices Italian bread
1 (12-ounce) can SPAM® Luncheon Meat, thinly sliced
¼ cup Dijon mustard
¼ cup thinly sliced green onions
4 (1-ounce) slices American cheese
2 tablespoons butter or margarine

Layer cheese and tomatoes evenly over 4 bread slices. Place SPAM® over tomatoes. Spread mustard on SPAM®. Sprinkle with onions. Top with American cheese and remaining 4 bread slices. In large skillet or griddle over medium heat, melt butter. Add sandwiches and cook until cheese is melted and sides are golden brown. Serve immediately.
Makes 4 servings

NUTRITIONAL INFORMATION PER SERVING:
Calories 613; Protein 34 g; Carbohydrates 38 g;
Fat 36 g; Cholesterol 136 mg; Sodium 1927 mg

Creamy SPAM™ Mushroom Sandwiches

1 (12-ounce) can SPAM® Luncheon Meat, finely cubed
1 (10¾-ounce) can 99% fat-free condensed cream of mushroom soup
½ cup (2 ounces) shredded Cheddar cheese
¼ cup chopped onion
12 slices bread, toasted

In medium bowl, combine SPAM®, soup, cheese and onion. Spread mixture on toasted bread. Place on baking sheet. Broil 4 to 5 minutes or until cheese is melted and bubbly. *Makes 12 servings*

NUTRITIONAL INFORMATION PER SERVING:
Calories 165; Protein 8 g; Carbohydrates 17 g;
Fat 7 g; Cholesterol 29 mg; Sodium 562 mg

Savory SPAM™ Crescents

10 slices bacon, cut into small pieces
¼ cup finely chopped onion
**1 (12-ounce) can SPAM® Luncheon
  Meat, cubed**
1 egg, beaten
3 tablespoons grated Parmesan cheese
2 tablespoons chopped fresh parsley
2 tablespoons Dijon mustard
⅛ teaspoon black pepper
**2 (8-ounce) packages refrigerated
  crescent roll dough**

Heat oven to 375°F. In large skillet, cook bacon and onion until bacon is crisp; drain. Stir in remaining ingredients except crescent roll dough. Separate each package of crescent dough into 8 triangles. Spread top half of each triangle with SPAM™ mixture; roll up. Place on baking sheets. Bake 12 to 15 minutes or until golden brown.   *Makes 16 servings*

NUTRITIONAL INFORMATION PER SERVING:
Calories 127; Protein 7 g; Carbohydrates 6 g;
Fat 9 g; Cholesterol 34 mg; Sodium 439 mg

SPAMBLED™ Egg Muffins

**1 (12-ounce) can SPAM® Luncheon
  Meat**
4 eggs, beaten
**4 English muffins, split and toasted
  Butter or margarine**
4 slices American cheese

Slice SPAM® into four square slices. In large skillet over medium heat, sauté SPAM® until lightly browned. Remove from skillet; set aside.

In same skillet, scramble eggs. Spread English muffins lightly with butter. Layer scrambled eggs, SPAM® slice and cheese slice on bottom half of each English muffin. Cover with top half of each muffin. Heat in microwave 30 seconds or in conventional oven 1 to 2 minutes or until cheese is melted.
    Makes 4 servings

NUTRITIONAL INFORMATION PER SERVING:
Calories 485; Protein 31 g; Carbohydrates 27 g;
Fat 27 g; Cholesterol 306 mg; Sodium 1687 mg

SPAM™ Breakfast Bagels

**1 (12-ounce) can SPAM® Luncheon
  Meat**
2 tablespoons butter or margarine
6 eggs, beaten
6 (1-ounce) slices American cheese
6 bagels, sliced

Slice SPAM® into 6 slices (3×¼-inch). In large skillet over medium heat, sauté SPAM® until lightly browned. Remove from skillet; keep warm. In same skillet, melt butter; pour in beaten eggs. Cook and stir to desired doneness. Layer scrambled eggs, SPAM® and cheese on bagel bottom. Cover with bagel top. Repeat with remaining bagels.
    Makes 6 servings

NUTRITIONAL INFORMATION PER SERVING:
Calories 504; Protein 29 g; Carbohydrates 36 g;
Fat 27 g; Cholesterol 294 mg; Sodium 1367 mg

Hero SPAM™ Sandwich

1 (16-ounce) loaf Italian bread
2 tablespoons Italian salad dressing
1 (12-ounce) can SPAM® Luncheon
   Meat, thinly sliced
1 tomato, thinly sliced
6 ounces sliced provolone cheese
1 (7-ounce) jar roasted red peppers,
   drained *or* 1 red bell pepper, cut
   into thin rings
1 small red onion, thinly sliced
10 pitted ripe olives, halved
   Lettuce leaves

Cut bread in half lengthwise; remove a
portion of soft center. Drizzle dressing
over cut sides of bread. Layer SPAM®,
tomato, cheese, peppers, onion, olives and
lettuce over bottom of loaf. Cover with
top half of bread; press down to make a
compact sandwich. Wrap in foil.
Refrigerate 2 hours. Cut crosswise to
serve.   *Makes 6 servings*

NUTRITIONAL INFORMATION PER SERVING:
Calories 364; Protein 20 g; Carbohydrates 27 g;
Fat 19 g; Cholesterol 65 mg; Sodium 1135 mg

SPAM™ Hot Vegetable Salad Sandwiches

6 unsliced whole wheat buns or Kaiser
   rolls
1 (7-ounce) can SPAM® Luncheon
   Meat, cubed
1 cup (4 ounces) shredded Monterey
   Jack cheese
1 tomato, chopped
½ cup finely chopped broccoli
½ cup thinly sliced carrots
¼ cup chopped onion
2 tablespoons peppercorn ranch-style
   salad dressing

Heat oven to 350°F. Cut thin slice from
top of each bun; reserve. Remove soft
center from each bun, leaving ½-inch
shell. Combine remaining ingredients.
Spoon into buns, pressing filling into
buns. Top with reserved bun tops. Wrap
each sandwich tightly in aluminum foil.
Bake 20 minutes or until thoroughly
heated and cheese is melted.

Makes 6 servings

NUTRITIONAL INFORMATION PER SERVING:
Calories 235; Protein 13 g; Carbohydrates 18 g;
Fat 13 g; Cholesterol 45 mg; Sodium 615 mg

Hero SPAM™ Sandwich

SPAM™ Pizza Pockets

1 (7-ounce) can SPAM® Luncheon
 Meat, cubed
1 small green bell pepper, chopped
1 small onion, chopped
½ cup chopped fresh mushrooms
1 (1-pound) loaf frozen bread dough,
 thawed
1 egg, beaten
1 tablespoon grated Parmesan cheese
¾ cup pizza sauce
1 teaspoon Italian seasoning

Heat oven to 350°F. In large skillet,
sauté SPAM®, bell pepper, onion and
mushrooms until lightly browned. Divide
bread dough into 6 equal parts. Roll into
6-inch circles. Brush circles with egg and
sprinkle with cheese. Divide SPAM™
mixture among bread circles. Top with 2
tablespoons pizza sauce. Sprinkle with
Italian seasoning. Fold circles in half.
Pinch edges together. Place on baking
sheet. Bake 20 to 25 minutes or until
golden brown.   *Makes 6 servings*

NUTRITIONAL INFORMATION PER SERVING:
Calories 328; Protein 13 g; Carbohydrates 43 g;
 Fat 11 g; Cholesterol 66 mg; Sodium 876 mg

SPAM™ Reuben Sandwiches

1 (8-ounce) can sauerkraut, drained
1 cup (4 ounces) shredded Swiss
 cheese
¼ cup Thousand Island salad dressing
8 slices rye bread
3 tablespoons butter or margarine,
 softened
1 (12-ounce) can SPAM® Luncheon
 Meat, cut into 8 slices

In small bowl, combine sauerkraut, cheese
and dressing. Spread one side of each
bread slice with butter. Spread half of
sauerkraut mixture on unbuttered side of
4 bread slices; top each with 2 slices
SPAM®. Cover with remaining sauerkraut
mixture. Top with remaining bread slices,
buttered side up. In large skillet or griddle
over medium heat, cook sandwiches until
cheese melts and both sides are golden
brown.   *Makes 4 servings*

NUTRITIONAL INFORMATION PER SERVING:
Calories 539; Protein 27 g; Carbohydrates 32 g;
 Fat 35 g; Cholesterol 121 mg; Sodium 1764 mg

SPAM™ Pizza Pocket

Maui SPAM™ Muffins

4 English muffins, split and toasted
Butter or margarine
Prepared mustard
1 (7-ounce) can SPAM® Luncheon
Meat, thinly sliced
1 (15¼-ounce) can pineapple slices,
drained
1 small green bell pepper, cut into
8 rings
¼ cup packed brown sugar
2 teaspoons water

Heat oven to 375°F. Spread muffin halves with butter and mustard. Layer SPAM® slices on each muffin half. Place 1 pineapple slice and 1 bell pepper ring on each muffin. Combine brown sugar and water; spoon over sandwiches. Place muffins on baking sheet. Bake 10 minutes. Serve hot. *Makes 8 servings*

NUTRITIONAL INFORMATION PER SERVING:
Calories 179; Protein 7 g; Carbohydrates 29 g;
Fat 4 g; Cholesterol 20 mg; Sodium 437 mg

Melted SPAM® & Cheese Poppy Seed Sandwiches

½ cup butter or margarine
3 tablespoons prepared mustard
1 tablespoon poppy seeds
8 slices cracked wheat bread
1 (12-ounce) can SPAM® Luncheon
Meat, cut into 8 slices
4 (1-ounce) slices American cheese

Heat oven to 375°F. In small bowl, combine butter, mustard and poppy seeds. Spread butter mixture on bread slices. Place 2 slices of SPAM® on each of 4 bread slices. Top SPAM® with 1 slice of cheese. Top with remaining 4 bread slices. Wrap sandwiches in foil. Bake 10 to 15 minutes or until cheese is melted.
Makes 4 servings

NUTRITIONAL INFORMATION PER SERVING:
Calories 626; Protein 25 g; Carbohydrates 28 g;
Fat 47 g; Cholesterol 157 mg; Sodium 1891 mg

Maui SPAM™ Muffins

Hearty Main Dishes

SPAM™ Lasagna

6 uncooked lasagna noodles
2½ cups chunky spaghetti sauce, divided
2 teaspoons dried basil leaves
1 (12-ounce) can SPAM® Luncheon Meat,
    thinly sliced, divided
2 cups (8 ounces) shredded mozzarella cheese,
    divided
⅓ cup grated Parmesan cheese

Heat oven to 350°F. Cook lasagna noodles according to package directions. In large bowl, combine spaghetti sauce and basil. In 9-inch square baking pan, spread ½ cup spaghetti sauce. Top with 3 lasagna noodles, cutting and overlapping noodles to fit, ½ of the SPAM® and ½ of the mozzarella cheese. Spread 1½ cups spaghetti sauce over mozzarella cheese. Repeat layers, ending with spaghetti sauce. Top with Parmesan cheese. Bake 45 to 50 minutes or until thoroughly heated.

Makes 6 servings

NUTRITIONAL INFORMATION PER SERVING:
Calories 444; Protein 25 g; Carbohydrates 39 g; Fat 21 g; Cholesterol 70 mg; Sodium 1333 mg

SPAM™ Confetti Pasta

Nonstick cooking spray
2 cups frozen whole kernel corn,
**   thawed**
1 (12-ounce) can SPAM® Luncheon
**   Meat, cut into 2-inch strips**
1 red bell pepper, chopped
1 green bell pepper, chopped
¾ cup chopped red onion
1½ cups whipping cream
2 tablespoons chili powder
¼ teaspoon black pepper
12 ounces angel hair pasta, cooked and
**   drained**
2 tomatoes, peeled and chopped
¼ cup minced fresh cilantro

In large skillet coated with cooking spray, sauté corn, SPAM®, bell peppers and onion over medium heat 5 minutes or until tender. Transfer mixture to bowl; keep warm. To same skillet, add cream, chili powder and black pepper. Bring to a boil; boil 5 minutes or until cream has thickened slightly, stirring occasionally. Pour over pasta and toss well. Spoon SPAM™ mixture over pasta. To serve, sprinkle with tomatoes and cilantro.

Makes 6 servings

NUTRITIONAL INFORMATION PER SERVING:
Calories 614; Protein 22 g; Carbohydrates 64 g;
Fat 32 g; Cholesterol 127 mg; Sodium 638 mg

The Original Baked SPAM®

1 (12-ounce) can SPAM® Luncheon
**   Meat**
Whole cloves
⅓ cup packed brown sugar
1 teaspoon water
1 teaspoon prepared mustard
½ teaspoon vinegar

Heat oven to 375°F. Place SPAM® on rack in shallow baking pan. Score surface; stud with cloves. In small bowl, combine brown sugar, water, mustard and vinegar, stirring until smooth. Brush glaze over SPAM®. Bake 20 minutes, basting often. Cut into slices to serve.   *Makes 6 servings*

NUTRITIONAL INFORMATION PER SERVING:
Calories 156; Protein 9 g; Carbohydrates 12 g;
Fat 8 g; Cholesterol 45 mg; Sodium 575 mg

SPAM™ Confetti Pasta

Baked SPAM® & Tortellini Casserole

1 (30-ounce) jar spaghetti sauce
1 (12-ounce) can SPAM® Luncheon Meat, cubed
1 (10-ounce) package refrigerated cheese tortellini
½ cup chopped onion
1 cup (4 ounces) shredded mozzarella cheese

Heat oven to 375°F. In 2½-quart casserole combine all ingredients except cheese; mix gently. Bake, covered, stirring halfway through baking, 50 to 60 minutes or until tortellini are tender. During last 5 minutes of baking, uncover and top with cheese. *Makes 6 servings*

NUTRITIONAL INFORMATION PER SERVING:
Calories 447; Protein 22 g; Carbohydrates 45 g; Fat 21 g; Cholesterol 74 mg; Sodium 1497 mg

SPAM™ Denver Biscuit Soufflé

1 (10-ounce) can refrigerated biscuits
3 eggs, separated
1 (3-ounce) package cream cheese, softened
1 (12-ounce) can SPAM® Luncheon Meat, cubed
1 cup (4 ounces) shredded Cheddar cheese
¼ cup chopped green bell pepper
¼ cup chopped onion
   Paprika

Heat oven to 350°F. Separate dough into 10 biscuits. Place biscuits in ungreased 9-inch round cake pan; press over bottom of pan to form crust. In medium bowl, beat egg yolks and cream cheese until smooth; stir in SPAM®, Cheddar cheese, bell pepper and onion. Beat egg whites until stiff; fold into SPAM™ mixture. Spoon evenly over crust. Sprinkle with paprika. Bake 45 to 50 minutes or until knife inserted near center comes out clean. Cut into wedges to serve.
Makes 6 servings

NUTRITIONAL INFORMATION PER SERVING:
Calories 385; Protein 20 g; Carbohydrates 18 g; Fat 25 g; Cholesterol 188 mg; Sodium 1166 mg

Creamy SPAM® & Broccoli with Pasta

6 ounces uncooked fettuccini pasta
1 (12-ounce) can SPAM® Luncheon Meat, cubed
1½ cups fresh or frozen broccoli florets
1 small onion, sliced, slices cut in half
1 tablespoon butter or margarine
1 (10-ounce) package refrigerated alfredo sauce

Cook pasta according to package directions. In large skillet, sauté SPAM®, broccoli and onion in butter until SPAM® is lightly browned and broccoli is crisp-tender. Stir in alfredo sauce. Cook, stirring constantly, until sauce is thoroughly heated. Serve over pasta.
Makes 6 servings

NUTRITIONAL INFORMATION PER SERVING:
Calories 384; Protein 19 g; Carbohydrates 19 g; Fat 26 g; Cholesterol 114 mg; Sodium 796 mg

Double Cheese SPAM™ Bake

       1 package active dry yeast
    ½ cup warm milk (120° to 130°F)
    ½ cup warm water (120° to 130°F)
       3 tablespoons butter or margarine, softened
       2 tablespoons sugar
       1 tablespoon dried parsley flakes
    ½ teaspoon salt
    ⅛ teaspoon garlic powder
       1 egg
    2¾ cups all-purpose flour, divided
       2 cups (8 ounces) shredded Cheddar cheese
       1 (12-ounce) can SPAM® Luncheon Meat, cut into strips
       1 cup (4 ounces) shredded mozzarella cheese
       2 tablespoons grated Parmesan or Romano cheese

In large bowl, dissolve yeast in warm milk and water. Add butter, sugar, parsley flakes, salt, garlic powder, egg and 1½ cups flour. Blend at low speed of electric mixer 30 seconds, scraping bowl constantly. Beat 3 minutes at high speed, scraping bowl occasionally. Stir in remaining 1¼ cups flour and Cheddar cheese until smooth. Cover; let rise in warm place until doubled in bulk, about 40 minutes.* Heat oven to 350°F. Spread dough in well-greased 12-inch pizza pan or 13×9-inch baking pan. Arrange SPAM® on top of dough, pressing down slightly. Bake 25 to 30 minutes or until golden brown. Sprinkle mozzarella and Parmesan cheeses over SPAM®. Bake 5 minutes longer or until cheese is melted.

Makes 6 servings

* The dough may be refrigerated 2 to 24 hours before baking.

NUTRITIONAL INFORMATION PER SERVING:
Calories 621; Protein 32 g; Carbohydrates 51 g; Fat 32 g; Cholesterol 149 mg; Sodium 1179 mg

SPAM™ Vegetable Hash

    ½ cup chopped onion
       2 tablespoons butter or margarine
       2 cups frozen cubed hash brown potatoes, thawed
       1 (12-ounce) can SPAM® Luncheon Meat, cubed
       1 (10-ounce) package frozen peas and carrots, thawed
    ½ teaspoon black pepper

In large skillet over medium-high heat, sauté onion in butter until tender. Stir in potatoes. Cook, stirring occasionally, until potatoes are lightly browned. Stir in SPAM®, peas and carrots and pepper. Cook, stirring occasionally, until thoroughly heated.

Makes 4 to 6 servings

NUTRITIONAL INFORMATION PER SERVING:
Calories 432; Protein 19 g; Carbohydrates 32 g; Fat 27 g; Cholesterol 83 mg; Sodium 982 mg

SPAM™ Fajitas

Nonstick cooking spray
1 green bell pepper, cut into julienne
strips
½ onion, cut into ¼-inch slices
1 (12-ounce) can SPAM® Luncheon
Meat, cut into julienne strips
¾ cup CHI-CHI'S® Salsa
8 (8-inch) flour tortillas, warmed
2 cups shredded lettuce
½ cup (2 ounces) shredded hot pepper
Monterey Jack or Cheddar cheese
½ cup nonfat plain yogurt
Additional CHI-CHI'S® Salsa
(optional)

Spray large nonstick skillet with cooking
spray. Heat skillet over medium-high
heat. Add green pepper and onion; sauté
2 minutes. Add SPAM®; sauté 2 minutes.
Stir in salsa and heat thoroughly. Spoon
about ½ cup SPAM™ mixture onto each
flour tortilla. Top each with ¼ cup
lettuce, 1 tablespoon cheese, 1 tablespoon
yogurt and salsa, if desired.

Makes 8 servings

NUTRITIONAL INFORMATION PER SERVING:
Calories 237; Protein 12 g; Carbohydrates 23 g;
Fat 11 g; Cholesterol 40 mg; Sodium 625 mg

SPAM™ Vegetable Casserole

2 (10¾-ounce) cans cream of
mushroom soup
½ cup milk
½ cup pasteurized processed cheese
spread
1 (16-ounce) package mixed frozen
vegetables, thawed
1 (12-ounce) can SPAM® Luncheon
Meat, cubed
1¼ cups uncooked instant rice
1 cup (4 ounces) shredded Cheddar
cheese
1 (2.8-ounce) can French-fried onions
2 cups crushed butter crackers
⅓ cup butter or margarine, melted

Heat oven to 350°F. In medium bowl,
combine soup, milk and cheese spread. In
large bowl, combine vegetables, SPAM®,
rice, cheese and onions; stir in soup
mixture. Pour into 13×9-inch baking
pan. Combine crackers and melted
butter; sprinkle over casserole. Bake 50 to
55 minutes or until hot.

Makes 8 servings

NUTRITIONAL INFORMATION PER SERVING:
Calories 371; Protein 13 g; Carbohydrates 30 g;
Fat 23 g; Cholesterol 60 mg; Sodium 1281 mg

SPAM™ Fajita

SPAM® à la King

⅓ cup chopped green bell pepper
3 tablespoons butter or margarine
3 tablespoons all-purpose flour
¼ teaspoon salt
⅛ teaspoon coarsely ground black pepper
1 cup water
1 cup half-and-half cream
1 HERB OX® Chicken-Flavored Bouillon Cube
1 (12-ounce) can SPAM® Luncheon Meat, cubed
1 (4-ounce) can sliced mushrooms, drained
¼ cup chopped pimiento
Puff pastry shells, rice or toast

In large saucepan, sauté bell pepper in butter until tender. Blend in flour, salt and black pepper until smooth. Stir in water, half-and-half and bouillon cube. Cook over low heat, stirring until bouillon dissolves and mixture boils and thickens. Add SPAM®, mushrooms and pimiento. Cook and stir 3 minutes. Serve over puff pastry shells.

Makes 4 servings

NUTRITIONAL INFORMATION PER SERVING:
Calories 354; Protein 17 g; Carbohydrates 9 g; Fat 28 g; Cholesterol 113 mg; Sodium 1366 mg

Pueblo SPAM®

2 cups cooked white rice
½ cup chopped fresh cilantro
1 (12-ounce) can SPAM® Luncheon Meat, cut into ¼-inch slices
1 onion, cut into wedges
2 cups (8 ounces) shredded Monterey Jack cheese with peppers
½ cup whipping cream
1 tablespoon vegetable oil
Warm tortillas

In medium bowl, combine rice and cilantro; set aside. In large skillet over medium-high heat, cook SPAM® and onion 7 to 10 minutes or until lightly browned. Meanwhile, in 2-quart saucepan over low heat, combine cheese, cream and oil. Cook, stirring occasionally, until cheese is melted. Place rice in center of plate; drizzle with cheese sauce. Place SPAM™ mixture around rice. Serve with warm tortillas.

Makes 4 servings

NUTRITIONAL INFORMATION PER SERVING:
Calories 657; Protein 31 g; Carbohydrates 33 g; Fat 44 g; Cholesterol 159 mg; Sodium 1159 mg

SPAM™ à la King

SPAM™ Skillet Dinner

3 medium zucchini
1 onion, thinly sliced
1 tablespoon vegetable oil
1 (12-ounce) can SPAM® Luncheon Meat
3 medium potatoes, peeled, sliced
3 carrots, peeled, sliced
1 (16-ounce) can chopped tomatoes
¾ teaspoon garlic powder
½ teaspoon dried basil leaves
½ teaspoon dried oregano leaves

Cut zucchini into ½-inch slices. In large skillet, sauté zucchini and onion in oil 5 minutes. Cut SPAM® into 8 slices; halve each slice. Add potatoes, carrots and SPAM® to skillet; pour tomatoes over SPAM®. Sprinkle with garlic, basil and oregano. Cover; simmer 25 minutes or until potatoes are tender, stirring occasionally.   *Makes 8 servings*

NUTRITIONAL INFORMATION PER SERVING:
Calories 191; Protein 9 g; Carbohydrates 21 g;
Fat 8 g; Cholesterol 34 mg; Sodium 527 mg

Elegant Potato SPAM™ Casserole

1 (10¾-ounce) can condensed cream of potato soup
¼ cup (1 ounce) grated Parmesan cheese, divided
2 tablespoons sherry
4 cups hot prepared mashed potatoes
   Nonstick cooking spray
1 (12-ounce) can SPAM® Luncheon Meat, cut into small pieces
¼ teaspoon paprika

Heat oven to 425°F. In small bowl, combine soup, 2 tablespoons cheese and sherry; stir until smooth. Spoon potatoes into 1½-quart casserole coated with cooking spray. Sprinkle SPAM® on top of potatoes. Spread soup mixture over SPAM®. Sprinkle remaining 2 tablespoons cheese and paprika over soup mixture. Bake 20 minutes or until thoroughly heated.   *Makes 8 servings*

NUTRITIONAL INFORMATION PER SERVING:
Calories 205; Protein 11 g; Carbohydrates 22 g;
Fat 8 g; Cholesterol 40 mg; Sodium 1100 mg

SPAM™ Enchiladas

1 (12-ounce) can SPAM® Luncheon Meat, finely chopped
1½ cups (6 ounces) shredded Monterey Jack cheese, divided
1½ cups (6 ounces) shredded Cheddar cheese, divided
1 green bell pepper, diced
½ cup chopped onion
1 cup CHI-CHI'S® Salsa, divided
8 (8-inch) flour tortillas
   Shredded lettuce
   Chopped tomato

Heat oven to 350°F. In medium bowl, combine SPAM®, 1 cup Monterey Jack cheese, 1 cup Cheddar cheese, bell pepper, onion and ¼ cup salsa. Spoon mixture down center of each tortilla; roll tightly. Place seam side down in 13×9-inch baking dish. Top with remaining salsa and cheese. Bake 20 minutes or until cheese is melted. Top with lettuce and tomato.   *Makes 4 servings*

NUTRITIONAL INFORMATION PER SERVING:
Calories 749; Protein 41 g; Carbohydrates 47 g;
Fat 46 g; Cholesterol 150 mg; Sodium 1657 mg

SPAM® & Creamy Noodle Bake

    6 ounces uncooked whole wheat noodles or egg noodles
    1 cup (4 ounces) ricotta cheese
    1 cup light sour cream
    ½ cup chopped onion
    ½ cup milk
    2 tablespoons butter or margarine, melted
    1 egg
    ¼ teaspoon ground nutmeg
    ¼ teaspoon black pepper
    1 (12-ounce) can SPAM® Luncheon Meat, cubed

Topping

    1 cup fresh torn bread cubes
    ⅓ cup grated Parmesan cheese
    2 tablespoons butter or margarine, melted
    1 tablespoon chopped fresh parsley *or* 1 teaspoon dried parsley leaves

Heat oven to 350°F. Cook noodles according to package directions. In large bowl, stir together ricotta cheese, sour cream, onion, milk, 2 tablespoons butter, egg, nutmeg and pepper. Stir in SPAM® and cooked noodles. Spoon mixture into greased 2½-quart casserole. Cover. Bake, stirring halfway through baking, 35 to 40 minutes or until thoroughly heated. In small bowl, combine all topping ingredients. During last 10 minutes of baking, uncover, stir and top with bread mixture. *Makes 6 servings*

NUTRITIONAL INFORMATION PER SERVING:
Calories 457; Protein 23 g; Carbohydrates 29 g; Fat 28 g; Cholesterol 161 mg; Sodium 841 mg

SPAM™ Swiss Pie

    1 (9-inch) deep-dish pie shell
    6 eggs, beaten
    1 cup whipping cream
    ⅛ teaspoon black pepper
    1 (12-ounce) can SPAM® Luncheon Meat, cubed
    ¼ cup chopped onion
    2 cups (8 ounces) shredded Swiss cheese, divided

Heat oven to 425°F. Bake pie shell 6 to 8 minutes. Remove from oven; *reduce oven temperature to 350°F.* In bowl, combine eggs, whipping cream and pepper. Stir in SPAM® and onion. Sprinkle 1 cup cheese in pie shell. Pour egg mixture over cheese. Sprinkle with remaining cheese. Bake 45 to 55 minutes or until set.

Makes 6 servings

NUTRITIONAL INFORMATION PER SERVING:
Calories 615; Protein 29 g; Carbohydrates 17 g; Fat 48 g; Cholesterol 346 mg; Sodium 920 mg

SPAM™ Cornbread Pie

    1 (8½-ounce) package cornbread mix
    1 (12-ounce) can SPAM® Luncheon Meat, cubed
    1½ cups (6 ounces) shredded Cheddar cheese

Heat oven to 400°F. Prepare cornbread mix according to package directions. Stir in SPAM®. Spread in 9-inch greased pie plate. Bake 15 to 20 minutes. Sprinkle with cheese. Bake 5 to 10 minutes or until cornbread is done. *Makes 6 servings*

NUTRITIONAL INFORMATION PER SERVING:
Calories 317; Protein 19 g; Carbohydrates 14 g; Fat 21 g; Cholesterol 102 mg; Sodium 1034 mg

SPAM™ Cakes

  1½ cups pancake mix
  1 cup milk
  1 egg
  1 tablespoon vegetable oil
  1 (7-ounce) can SPAM® Luncheon
      Meat, finely chopped
  Syrup or honey

In large bowl, combine pancake mix, milk, egg and oil. Stir in SPAM®. Using ⅓ cup for each pancake, pour batter onto greased griddle; cook until browned on bottom. Turn and cook until browned. Serve with syrup or honey.

Makes 6 servings (12 pancakes)

NUTRITIONAL INFORMATION PER SERVING
Calories 237; Protein 11 g; Carbohydrates 28 g;
Fat 9 g; Cholesterol 65 mg; Sodium 841 mg

SPAM™ Sticks

  1 (12-ounce) can SPAM® Luncheon
      Meat
  1 egg
  2 tablespoons milk
  2 tablespoons all-purpose flour
  ½ cup soda cracker crumbs
  Tartar sauce or ketchup

Heat oven to 375°F. Slice SPAM® into 8 pieces; cut each slice in half lengthwise. Beat together egg and milk. Coat each SPAM® slice with flour. Dip in milk mixture and roll in cracker crumbs. Place on baking sheet. Bake 15 to 18 minutes or until golden brown. Serve with tartar sauce or ketchup.   *Makes 4 servings*

NUTRITIONAL INFORMATION PER SERVING:
Calories 251; Protein 17 g; Carbohydrates 13 g;
Fat 14 g; Cholesterol 122 mg; Sodium 952 mg

SPAM® & Black Beans with Rice

  1 cup uncooked long grain rice
  1 (12-ounce) can SPAM® Luncheon
      Meat, cubed
  ½ cup chopped onion
  ½ cup chopped green bell pepper
  1 tablespoon butter or margarine
  1 (15-ounce) can black beans, drained
  1 (15-ounce) can Cajun-style stewed
      tomatoes
  ½ teaspoon cumin
  ⅛ teaspoon cayenne pepper

Cook rice according to package directions. In large skillet, sauté SPAM®, onion and bell pepper in butter until onion is softened and SPAM® is lightly browned. Stir in beans, tomatoes, cumin and cayenne pepper. Cook, stirring occasionally, until beans are thoroughly heated. Serve over rice.

Makes 6 servings

NUTRITIONAL INFORMATION PER SERVING:
Calories 453; Protein 25 g; Carbohydrates 64 g;
Fat 11 g; Cholesterol 50 mg; Sodium 594 mg

SPAM™ Cakes

SPAM® & Pasta Stuffed Tomatoes

1 (7¼-ounce) package macaroni and cheese
8 medium tomatoes
1 (12-ounce) can SPAM® Luncheon Meat, cubed
2 tablespoons chopped fresh chives *or* **1 tablespoon dried chives**
1 tablespoon chopped fresh basil *or* **1 teaspoon dried basil leaves**
½ teaspoon onion powder
¼ teaspoon black pepper

Prepare macaroni and cheese according to package directions. Meanwhile, cut tops off tomatoes; scoop out pulp. Place tomatoes, cut side down, on paper towels to drain. Heat oven to 350°F. In large bowl, combine prepared macaroni and cheese, SPAM®, chives and basil; mix well. In small bowl, combine onion powder and pepper; sprinkle inside of drained tomatoes with onion mixture. Spoon macaroni and cheese mixture into tomatoes. Place filled tomatoes in lightly greased 13×9-inch baking pan. Cover. Bake 20 to 25 minutes or until tomatoes are tender and thoroughly heated.

Makes 8 servings

NUTRITIONAL INFORMATION PER SERVING:
Calories 165; Protein 10 g; Carbohydrates 11 g; Fat 9 g; Cholesterol 39 mg; Sodium 571 mg

SPAM® & Gravy on Biscuits

1 (17.3-ounce) can refrigerated large buttermilk biscuits
1 (12-ounce) can SPAM® Luncheon Meat, cubed
¼ cup chopped onion
2 tablespoons butter or margarine
2 tablespoons all-purpose flour
¼ teaspoon black pepper
2 cups milk

Prepare biscuits according to package directions. In large skillet over medium-high heat, sauté SPAM® and onion in butter until SPAM® is lightly browned. Stir in flour and pepper. Cook 1 minute, stirring constantly. Stir in milk. Cook, stirring occasionally, until mixture just comes to a boil. Reduce heat to medium. Cook, stirring occasionally, until gravy is thickened. Serve over hot biscuits.

Makes 8 servings

NUTRITIONAL INFORMATION PER SERVING:
Calories 347; Protein 13 g; Carbohydrates 35 g; Fat 17 g; Cholesterol 49 mg; Sodium 1243 mg

SPAM® & Pasta Stuffed Tomatoes

SPAM™ Cheesy Broccoli Bake

1 (10-ounce) package frozen chopped broccoli
1 (10³/₄-ounce) can Cheddar cheese soup
¹/₂ cup sour cream
1 (12-ounce) can SPAM® Luncheon Meat, cubed
1¹/₂ cups cooked white rice
¹/₂ cup buttered bread crumbs

Heat oven to 350°F. Cook broccoli according to package directions. Drain well. In medium bowl, combine soup and sour cream. Add broccoli, SPAM® and rice to soup mixture. Spoon into 1¹/₂-quart casserole. Sprinkle with bread crumbs. Bake 30 to 35 minutes or until thoroughly heated.

Makes 4 to 6 servings

NUTRITIONAL INFORMATION PER SERVING:
Calories 493; Protein 23 g; Carbohydrates 42 g; Fat 26 g; Cholesterol 101 mg; Sodium 1545 mg

SPAM™ Strudels with Mustard Sauce

1 (12-ounce) can SPAM® Luncheon Meat, chopped
1 cup (4 ounces) shredded Swiss cheese
1 cup sliced fresh mushrooms
¹/₄ cup chopped green onions
1 egg, beaten
8 frozen phyllo leaves, thawed
¹/₂ cup butter or margarine, melted Mustard Sauce (recipe follows)

Heat oven to 350°F. In large bowl, combine SPAM®, cheese, mushrooms, onions and egg. Brush 1 phyllo sheet with butter. (Keep remaining phyllo covered with damp towel to prevent drying.) Fold sheet in half crosswise; brush with butter. Fold in half crosswise again; brush with butter. Place ¹/₃ cup SPAM™ mixture in center of sheet. Fold long sides up and over filling, overlapping slightly. Fold into thirds from narrow edge. Place seam side down on baking sheet. (Cover with damp towel to prevent drying.) Repeat with remaining phyllo sheets. Bake 20 minutes or until golden. Serve with Mustard Sauce.

Makes 8 servings

Mustard Sauce

In small saucepan, combine ¹/₂ cup sour cream, ¹/₂ cup mayonnaise or salad dressing, 1 tablespoon dry mustard and ¹/₂ teaspoon sugar. Heat over low heat, stirring occasionally, until warm.

NUTRITIONAL INFORMATION PER SERVING:
Calories 444; Protein 15 g; Carbohydrates 16 g; Fat 37 g; Cholesterol 119 mg; Sodium 816 mg

Enchilada Breakfast SPAM™ Casserole

8 (8-inch) flour tortillas
1 (12-ounce) can SPAM® Luncheon Meat, cubed
1 cup chopped onions
1 cup chopped green bell pepper
1 tomato, chopped
2 cups (8 ounces) shredded Cheddar cheese, divided
4 eggs
2 cups whipping cream
1 (4.25-ounce) jar CHI-CHI'S® Diced Green Chilies
CHI-CHI'S® Picante Sauce

In center of each tortilla, place about ¼ cup SPAM®, 1 tablespoon onion, 1 tablespoon bell pepper, 1 tablespoon tomato and 1 tablespoon cheese. Roll up tightly. Repeat procedure to make 8 enchiladas. Place enchiladas seam side down in greased 13×9-inch baking dish. In medium bowl, beat together eggs, cream and green chilies. Pour over enchiladas. Cover. Refrigerate overnight. Heat oven to 350°F. Bake, uncovered, 40 to 50 minutes or until egg mixture is set. Sprinkle with remaining cheese. Bake 5 minutes longer or until cheese is melted. Serve with picante sauce.

Makes 8 servings

NUTRITIONAL INFORMATION PER SERVING:
Calories 565; Protein 21 g; Carbohydrates 27 g; Fat 43 g; Cholesterol 251 mg; Sodium 952 mg

Hearty SPAM™ Breakfast Skillet

2 cups frozen diced or shredded potatoes, thawed
½ cup chopped onion
¼ medium green bell pepper, cut into 1-inch thin strips
¼ medium red or yellow bell pepper, cut into 1-inch thin strips
2 teaspoons vegetable oil
1 (12-ounce) can SPAM® Luncheon Meat, cut into julienne strips
1 (8-ounce) carton frozen fat-free egg product, thawed *or* 4 eggs
¼ teaspoon dried basil leaves
⅛ teaspoon salt
⅛ teaspoon black pepper
6 drops hot pepper sauce
¼ cup (1 ounce) shredded Cheddar cheese

In large nonstick skillet over medium-high heat, cook potatoes, onion and bell peppers in oil 5 minutes, stirring constantly. Add SPAM®; cook and stir 5 minutes. In small bowl, combine egg product, basil, salt, black pepper and hot pepper sauce; blend well. Pour over mixture in skillet. Cover. Cook over medium-low heat 8 to 12 minutes or until set. Sprinkle with cheese; remove from heat.   *Makes 6 servings*

NUTRITIONAL INFORMATION PER SERVING:
Calories 294; Protein 17 g; Carbohydrates 17 g; Fat 18 g; Cholesterol 50 mg; Sodium 725 mg

SPAM™ Hawaiian Pizza

**1 (10-ounce) can refrigerated pizza
crust**
**1 (6-ounce) package sliced provolone
cheese**
**1 (12-ounce) can SPAM® Luncheon
Meat, cut into thin squares**
**1 (8-ounce) can chunk pineapple,
drained**
½ cup thinly sliced red onion rings
½ cup chopped green bell pepper

Heat oven to 425°F. Grease 12-inch pizza
pan or 13×9-inch baking pan. Unroll
dough; press into prepared pan. Top with
cheese. Arrange remaining ingredients
over cheese. Bake 25 to 30 minutes or
until crust is deep golden brown.
Makes 6 servings

NUTRITIONAL INFORMATION PER SERVING:
Calories 373; Protein 20 g; Carbohydrates 30 g;
Fat 21 g; Cholesterol 65 mg; Sodium 1192 mg

SPAM™ Corn Pudding

**1 (12-ounce) can SPAM® Luncheon
Meat, cubed**
⅓ cup chopped green bell pepper
¼ cup chopped onion
2 tablespoons butter or margarine
6 eggs
2 cups milk
1 tablespoon all-purpose flour
2 teaspoons sugar
1 teaspoon salt
⅛ teaspoon black pepper
**2 (10-ounce) packages frozen whole
kernel corn, thawed and drained**

Heat oven to 300°F. In large skillet, sauté
SPAM®, bell pepper and onion in butter
until tender. In large bowl, beat eggs.
Stir in milk, flour, sugar, salt and black
pepper. Add SPAM™ mixture and corn.
Pour into greased 12×8-inch baking
dish. Bake 1 hour and 10 minutes or
until set. *Makes 8 servings*

NUTRITIONAL INFORMATION PER SERVING:
Calories 232; Protein 14 g; Carbohydrates 18 g;
Fat 13 g; Cholesterol 201 mg; Sodium 767 mg

SPAM™ Hawaiian Pizza

Maple SPAM™ Stuffed Squash

3 small acorn squash (about 1 pound each), cut in half, seeds removed
½ cup chopped celery
¼ cup chopped onion
2 tablespoons butter or margarine
1 (12-ounce) can SPAM® Luncheon Meat, chopped
1½ cups frozen cubed hash brown potatoes, thawed
½ cup chopped apple
¼ cup pure maple syrup or maple-flavored syrup

Heat oven to 375°F. Place squash, cut side up, in 13×9-inch baking pan. In large skillet over medium-high heat, sauté celery and onion in butter until tender. Stir in SPAM® and potatoes. Cook, stirring occasionally, until potatoes are lightly browned. Stir in apple and syrup. Spoon ½ cup SPAM™ mixture into each squash half. Cover. Bake 40 to 50 minutes or until squash is tender.

Makes 6 servings

NUTRITIONAL INFORMATION PER SERVING:
Calories 363; Protein 12 g; Carbohydrates 46 g; Fat 17 g; Cholesterol 55 mg; Sodium 630 mg

SPAM™ Potatoes Alfredo

4 baking potatoes
1 tablespoon butter or margarine
½ cup chopped green onions
1 (12-ounce) can SPAM® Luncheon Meat, diced
1 (8-ounce) package cream cheese, softened and cubed
⅔ cup milk
½ teaspoon black pepper

Heat oven to 400°F. Wrap potatoes in foil. Bake 1 hour or until tender. Meanwhile, in large saucepan, melt butter. Add green onions. Cook, stirring constantly, 2 minutes or until tender. Add SPAM®, cream cheese, milk and pepper. Cook, stirring constantly, until cheese is melted. Split potatoes. Serve sauce over potatoes. *Makes 4 servings*

NUTRITIONAL INFORMATION PER SERVING:
Calories 633; Protein 24 g; Carbohydrates 56 g; Fat 36 g; Cholesterol 141 mg; Sodium 1046 mg

Maple SPAM™ Stuffed Squash

Cheesy Country SPAM™ Puff

6 slices white bread, torn into small pieces
1¼ cups milk
3 eggs
1 tablespoon spicy mustard
½ teaspoon garlic powder
½ teaspoon paprika
1 (12-ounce) can SPAM® Luncheon Meat, cubed
2 cups (8 ounces) shredded sharp Cheddar cheese, divided
½ cup chopped onion
½ cup (2 ounces) shredded Monterey Jack cheese

Heat oven to 375°F. In large bowl, combine bread, milk, eggs, mustard, garlic powder and paprika. Beat at medium speed of electric mixer 1 minute or until smooth. Stir in SPAM®, 1 cup Cheddar cheese and onion. Pour into greased 12×8-inch baking dish. Bake 25 minutes. Top with remaining 1 cup Cheddar cheese and Monterey Jack cheese. Bake 5 minutes longer or until cheese is melted. Let stand 10 minutes before serving.

Makes 6 servings

NUTRITIONAL INFORMATION PER SERVING:
Calories 434; Protein 28 g; Carbohydrates 19 g; Fat 28 g; Cholesterol 203 mg; Sodium 1077 mg

SPAM™ Hash Brown Bake

1 (32-ounce) package frozen hash brown potatoes, thawed slightly
½ cup butter or margarine, melted
1 teaspoon salt
1 teaspoon black pepper
½ teaspoon garlic powder
2 cups (8 ounces) shredded Cheddar cheese
1 (12-ounce) can SPAM® Luncheon Meat, cubed
1 (10¾-ounce) can cream of chicken soup
1½ cups sour cream
½ cup milk
½ cup chopped onion
1 (4.25-ounce) jar CHI-CHI'S® Diced Green Chilies, drained
2 cups crushed potato chips

Heat oven to 350°F. In large bowl, combine potatoes, melted butter, salt, pepper and garlic powder. In separate large bowl, combine cheese, SPAM®, soup, sour cream, milk, onion and green chilies. Add SPAM™ mixture to potato mixture; mix well. Pour into 2-quart baking dish. Sprinkle with potato chips. Bake 45 to 60 minutes or until thoroughly heated. *Makes 8 servings*

NUTRITIONAL INFORMATION PER SERVING:
Calories 705; Protein 21 g; Carbohydrates 41 g; Fat 53 g; Cholesterol 118 mg; Sodium 1447 mg

Cheesy Country SPAM™ Puff

French Fry SPAM™ Casserole

1 (20-ounce) bag frozen French fried
    potatoes, thawed
2 cups (8 ounces) shredded Cheddar
    cheese
2 cups sour cream
1 (10¾-ounce) can condensed cream
    of chicken soup
1 (12-ounce) can SPAM® Luncheon
    Meat, cubed
½ cup chopped red bell pepper
½ cup chopped green onions
½ cup finely crushed corn flakes

Heat oven to 350°F. In large bowl,
combine potatoes, cheese, sour cream and
soup. Stir in SPAM®, bell pepper and
green onions. Spoon into 13×9-inch
baking dish. Sprinkle with corn flakes.
Bake 30 to 40 minutes or until
thoroughly heated.

Makes 6 to 8 servings

NUTRITIONAL INFORMATION PER SERVING:
Calories 786; Protein 26 g; Carbohydrates 49 g;
Fat 55 g; Cholesterol 122 mg; Sodium 1476 mg

SPAM™ Fried Rice

2 tablespoons vegetable oil, divided
2 eggs, beaten
1 (12-ounce) can SPAM® Luncheon
    Meat, cubed
¼ cup finely chopped fresh mushrooms
¼ cup chopped green onions
2 cups cooked white rice
3 tablespoons HOUSE OF TSANG®
    Soy Sauce

In large skillet, heat 1 tablespoon oil. Add
eggs; cook and stir to desired doneness.
Remove from skillet. In same skillet, heat
remaining 1 tablespoon oil. Add SPAM®,
mushrooms and green onions; cook
4 minutes or until vegetables are tender.
Stir in rice and egg. Sprinkle with soy
sauce. Heat thoroughly.

Makes 4 to 6 servings

NUTRITIONAL INFORMATION PER SERVING:
Calories 405; Protein 20 g; Carbohydrates 31 g;
Fat 22 g; Cholesterol 174 mg; Sodium 1646 mg

SPAM™ Breakfast Burritos

1 (12-ounce) can SPAM® Luncheon
   Meat, cubed
4 eggs
2 tablespoons milk
1 tablespoon butter or margarine
6 (6-inch) flour tortillas
1 cup (4 ounces) shredded Cheddar
   cheese, divided
1 cup (4 ounces) shredded Monterey
   Jack cheese, divided
CHI-CHI'S® Salsa or Taco Sauce

Heat oven to 400°F. In medium bowl,
beat together SPAM®, eggs and milk.
Melt butter in large skillet; add egg
mixture. Cook, stirring, to desired
doneness. Divide SPAM™ mixture and
half of cheeses over tortillas. Roll up
burritos; place seam side down in 12×8-
inch baking dish. Sprinkle remaining
cheeses over top of burritos. Bake 5 to 10
minutes or until cheese is melted. Serve
with salsa.   *Makes 6 servings*

NUTRITIONAL INFORMATION PER SERVING:
Calories 430; Protein 25 g; Carbohydrates 20 g;
Fat 28 g; Cholesterol 562 mg; Sodium 976 mg

SPAM® and Rice Casserole

1 (12-ounce) can SPAM® Luncheon
   Meat, cubed
2 cups cooked white rice
½ cup chopped water chestnuts
½ cup sliced celery
¼ cup sliced green onions
¼ teaspoon black pepper
1 (10¾-ounce) can cream of
   mushroom soup
⅓ cup mayonnaise or salad dressing

Heat oven to 350°F. In medium bowl,
combine SPAM®, rice, celery, water
chestnuts, green onions and pepper. In
small bowl, combine soup and
mayonnaise; mix with SPAM™ mixture.
Spoon into 1½-quart casserole. Bake 35
to 40 minutes or until thoroughly heated.
          Makes 4 to 6 servings

NUTRITIONAL INFORMATION PER SERVING:
Calories 541; Protein 20 g; Carbohydrates 43 g;
Fat 33 g; Cholesterol 79 mg; Sodium 1582 mg

Light Main Dishes

SPAM™ Hot & Spicy Stir-Fry

⅓ cup reduced sodium teriyaki sauce
⅓ cup water
2 to 3 teaspoons HOUSE OF TSANG®
  Chinese Hot Oil
½ teaspoon ground ginger
1 (12-ounce) can SPAM® Lite Luncheon
  Meat, cubed
1 cup broccoli florets
1 cup chopped onion
1 cup pea pods
1 red bell pepper, cut into strips
1½ tablespoons vegetable oil
1 (14-ounce) can whole baby corn, drained
  and cut in half
1 (7-ounce) jar mushrooms, drained
6 cups hot cooked white rice

In small bowl, combine teriyaki sauce, water, Chinese hot oil and ginger; set aside. In wok or large skillet, stir-fry SPAM®, broccoli, onion, pea pods and bell pepper in oil 2 minutes. Add teriyaki sauce mixture; cook until bubbly. Add baby corn and mushrooms; heat thoroughly. Serve over rice.   *Makes 6 servings*

NUTRITIONAL INFORMATION PER SERVING:
Calories 521; Protein 19 g; Carbohydrates 80 g; Fat 14 g; Cholesterol 45 mg; Sodium 1120 mg

Creamy SPAM™ Broccoli Casserole

Nonstick cooking spray
1 (7-ounce) package elbow macaroni
2 cups frozen cut broccoli, thawed and drained
1 (12-ounce) can SPAM® Lite Luncheon Meat, cubed
½ cup chopped red bell pepper
2 cups skim milk
2 tablespoons cornstarch
¼ teaspoon black pepper
1 cup (4 ounces) shredded fat free Cheddar cheese
¾ cup soft bread crumbs
2 teaspoons margarine, melted

Heat oven to 350°F. Spray 2-quart casserole with nonstick cooking spray. Cook macaroni according to package directions; drain. In prepared casserole, combine macaroni, broccoli, SPAM® and bell pepper. In small saucepan, stir together milk, cornstarch and black pepper until cornstarch is dissolved. Bring to a boil, stirring constantly, until thickened. Reduce heat to low. Add cheese; stir until melted. Stir sauce into SPAM™ mixture. Combine bread crumbs and margarine; sprinkle on top of casserole. Bake 40 minutes or until thoroughly heated. *Makes 8 servings*

NUTRITIONAL INFORMATION PER SERVING:
Calories 263; Protein 18 g; Carbohydrates 30g; Fat 8 g; Cholesterol 37 mg; Sodium 632 mg

New-Fashioned SPAM™ Scalloped Potatoes

Nonstick cooking spray
1 (10¾-ounce) can 99% fat-free condensed cream of mushroom soup
½ cup skim milk
1 (2-ounce) jar diced pimiento, drained
¼ teaspoon black pepper
1 (12-ounce) can SPAM® Lite Luncheon Meat, cubed
1 cup chopped onion
½ cup frozen peas
4½ cups thinly sliced, peeled potatoes
2 tablespoons dry bread crumbs
1 tablespoon chopped fresh parsley

Preheat oven to 350°F. Spray 2-quart casserole with nonstick cooking spray. In medium bowl, combine soup, milk, pimiento and pepper. In casserole, layer half of each of SPAM®, onion, peas, potatoes and sauce. Repeat layers. Cover. Bake 1 hour or until potatoes are nearly tender. Combine bread crumbs and parsley; sprinkle over casserole. Bake, uncovered, 15 minutes longer or until potatoes are tender. Let stand 10 minutes before serving. *Makes 6 servings*

NUTRITIONAL INFORMATION PER SERVING:
Calories 276; Protein 13 g; Carbohydrates 35g; Fat 9 g; Cholesterol 48 mg; Sodium 826 mg

Creamy SPAM™ Broccoli Casserole

SPAM™ Stuffed Potatoes Florentine

Nonstick cooking spray
1 (12-ounce) can SPAM® Lite Luncheon Meat, cubed
1 teaspoon butter or margarine
⅓ cup chopped onion
½ (10-ounce) package frozen chopped spinach, thawed and squeezed dry
¼ teaspoon dried thyme leaves
6 baking potatoes, baked and kept warm
¼ cup skim milk
2 tablespoons grated Parmesan cheese
¼ teaspoon black pepper
¼ cup (1 ounce) shredded Monterey Jack cheese
¼ cup (1 ounce) shredded Cheddar cheese

Heat oven to 350°F. Spray shallow rectangular 2-quart baking dish with nonstick cooking spray. In large nonstick skillet, sauté SPAM® in butter 3 minutes. Add onion, spinach and thyme; cook and stir 2 minutes. Set aside. Cut thin slice off top of each potato. Scoop out each potato, leaving ½-inch shell.

Place shells in prepared baking dish. Place scooped out potato in medium bowl. Beat at medium speed of electric mixer 30 seconds. Add milk, Parmesan cheese and pepper; beat just until combined. Stir in SPAM™ mixture. Fill potato shells with potato mixture. Bake, uncovered, 25 to 30 minutes or until thoroughly heated. Top with cheeses. Bake 5 minutes longer or until cheese is melted. *Makes 6 servings*

NUTRITIONAL INFORMATION PER SERVING:
Calories 396; Protein 18 g; Carbohydrates 54g; Fat 12 g; Cholesterol 56 mg; Sodium 704 mg

Spicy SPAM™ Kabobs

¼ cup lemon juice
3 tablespoons minced onion
1 tablespoon olive oil
1 clove garlic, minced
1 teaspoon dried thyme leaves
½ teaspoon dried oregano leaves
¼ teaspoon crushed red pepper
16 pea pods
1 (8-ounce) can pineapple chunks packed in its own juice, drained
1 (12-ounce) can SPAM® Lite Luncheon Meat, cut into 24 cubes
1 red bell pepper, cut into 1-inch pieces
4 cups hot cooked white rice

Combine lemon juice, onion, olive oil, garlic, thyme, oregano and crushed red pepper in 13×9-inch dish. Wrap pea pods around pineapple chunks. Alternately thread SPAM® cubes, pineapple chunks and bell pepper pieces onto eight skewers. Place in dish with marinade. Cover and marinate 2 hours, turning occasionally. Grill kabobs over medium-hot coals 10 minutes, turning occasionally. Or, broil 5 inches from heat source 8 to 10 minutes, turning occasionally. Serve with rice.

Makes 4 servings

NUTRITIONAL INFORMATION PER SERVING:
Calories 536; Protein 22 g; Carbohydrates 75g; Fat 16 g; Cholesterol 68 mg; Sodium 848 mg

Spicy SPAM™ Kabobs

SPAM™ Fettuccini Primavera

1 tablespoon butter or margarine
2 tablespoons all-purpose flour
1½ cups skim milk
½ cup low sodium chicken broth
1½ teaspoons dried basil leaves
12 ounces uncooked fettuccini
1 (12-ounce) can SPAM® Lite
  Luncheon Meat, cut into julienne
  strips
1 (16-ounce) package frozen broccoli,
  carrot and cauliflower
  combination, cooked and drained
⅔ cup grated Parmesan cheese

In small saucepan, melt butter. Stir in flour. Cook and stir 1 minute. Stir in milk, chicken broth and basil. Bring to a boil, stirring constantly, until thickened; keep warm. In 5-quart saucepan, cook fettuccini according to package directions; drain and return to saucepan. Stir in SPAM®, vegetables and sauce. Cook and stir over medium-high heat until thoroughly heated. Stir in Parmesan cheese. *Makes 6 to 8 servings*

NUTRITIONAL INFORMATION PER SERVING:
Calories 441; Protein 26 g; Carbohydrates 51g;
Fat 14 g; Cholesterol 55 mg; Sodium 909 mg

Vegetable SPAM™ Stuffed Acorn Squash

3 (1-pound) acorn squash
1 (12-ounce) can SPAM® Lite
  Luncheon Meat, cubed
½ cup diced red bell pepper
½ cup diced jicama
½ cup finely chopped onion
2 small tomatoes, peeled and finely
  diced
½ teaspoon coarsely ground black
  pepper
½ cup HOUSE OF TSANG® Ginger
  Soy Sauce
¼ cup chopped green onions

Heat oven to 400°F. Lightly coat 13×9-inch baking pan with cooking spray. Cut squash in half lengthwise; remove seeds. Place squash, cut sides down, in pan. Bake 40 minutes or until tender. Meanwhile, in large skillet over medium-high heat, sauté SPAM® 2 to 3 minutes or until lightly browned. Remove from skillet. Add bell pepper, jicama, onion, tomatoes and black pepper. Cook 5 minutes, stirring frequently. Add soy sauce. Bring to a boil. Return SPAM® to skillet. Heat thoroughly. Fill each squash cavity with SPAM™ mixture. Sprinkle with green onions. *Makes 6 servings*

NUTRITIONAL INFORMATION PER SERVING:
Calories 235; Protein 13 g; Carbohydrates 31g;
Fat 8 g; Cholesterol 45 mg; Sodium 1372 mg

SPAM™ Fettuccini Primavera

SPAM™ Skillet Casserole

2 baking potatoes, cut into ⅛-inch
    slices
1 (12-ounce) can SPAM® Lite
    Luncheon Meat, cubed
1 cup thinly sliced carrots
1 cup thinly sliced onions
½ cup thinly sliced celery
2 cloves garlic, minced
2 tablespoons all-purpose flour
1 teaspoon coarsely ground black
    pepper
¾ teaspoon dried thyme leaves
1 (16-ounce) can no-salt-added green
    beans, drained
1 (16-ounce) can no-salt-added whole
    tomatoes, drained and chopped
1 (5½-ounce) can no-salt-added
    vegetable juice cocktail
    Butter-flavored nonstick cooking
    spray

Cook potatoes in boiling water 3 minutes
or until crisp-tender. Drain. In large
skillet, cook SPAM® until browned;
remove from skillet. Add carrots to
skillet; sauté 4 to 5 minutes. Add onions,
celery and garlic; sauté until tender.
Combine flour, pepper and thyme. Stir
flour mixture into vegetable mixture; cook
1 minute, stirring constantly. Add
SPAM®, green beans, tomatoes and
vegetable juice cocktail. Bring to a boil.
Reduce heat; simmer 5 minutes, stirring
occasionally. Remove skillet from heat;
arrange potato slices over top. Spray
potato slices with cooking spray. Broil 6
inches from heat source 10 minutes or
until golden.   *Makes 6 servings*

NUTRITIONAL INFORMATION PER SERVING:
Calories 245; Protein 13 g; Carbohydrates 31g;
Fat 8 g; Cholesterol 45 mg; Sodium 683 mg

Healthy SPAM™ Peppers

1 (12-ounce) can SPAM® Lite
    Luncheon Meat, cubed
2 cups shredded cabbage
1 cup shredded zucchini
1 onion, shredded
1 carrot, shredded
2 cloves garlic, minced
1½ tablespoons chopped fresh basil
1 teaspoon dried oregano leaves
½ teaspoon crushed red pepper
1 (28-ounce) can diced tomatoes
1½ cups instant rice
1 tablespoon brown sugar
10 green bell peppers, cored and seeded

In large skillet over medium-high heat,
sauté SPAM® until lightly browned;
remove from skillet. Add cabbage,
zucchini, onion, carrot, garlic, basil,
oregano and crushed red pepper to skillet.
Cook over low heat 10 minutes or until
vegetables are crisp-tender. Drain juice
from tomatoes; reserve juice. Add enough
water to tomato juice to equal 2 cups.
Add juice mixture, tomatoes, SPAM®,
rice and brown sugar to vegetable mixture.
Cover. Cook 10 minutes. In large
saucepan, boil bell peppers in water 5 to 7
minutes or until crisp-tender. Drain. Fill
peppers with SPAM™ mixture.
          Makes 10 servings

NUTRITIONAL INFORMATION PER SERVING:
Calories 176; Protein 9 g; Carbohydrates 25 g;
Fat 5 g; Cholesterol 27 mg; Sodium 355 mg

Healthy SPAM™ Pepper

SPAM™ Jambalaya

1 (12-ounce) can SPAM® Lite Luncheon Meat, cubed
1 cup chopped onion
⅔ cup chopped green bell pepper
½ cup chopped celery
2 cloves garlic, minced
1 (14½-ounce) can tomatoes, cut up
1 (10¾-ounce) can low sodium chicken broth
½ teaspoon dried thyme leaves
6 to 8 drops hot pepper sauce
1 bay leaf
1 cup long-grain rice
2 tablespoons chopped fresh parsley

In large nonstick skillet or 3-quart nonstick saucepan, sauté SPAM®, onion, bell pepper, celery and garlic until vegetables are tender. Add tomatoes, chicken broth, thyme, hot pepper sauce and bay leaf. Bring to a boil; stir in rice. Cover. Reduce heat and simmer 20 minutes or until rice is tender. Discard bay leaf. Sprinkle with parsley.

Makes 6 servings

NUTRITIONAL INFORMATION PER SERVING:
Calories 261; Protein 13 g; Carbohydrates 32 g; Fat 8 g; Cholesterol 45 mg; Sodium 850 mg

SPAM™ Carbonara

1 onion, finely chopped
½ teaspoon fennel seeds
1¾ cups chicken broth, divided
1 (12-ounce) can SPAM® Lite Luncheon Meat, cut into strips
1 cup finely chopped fresh parsley
3 egg whites
1 egg
1 (16-ounce) package vermicelli
1½ cups (6 ounces) shredded Parmesan cheese, divided

In large nonstick skillet, combine onion, fennel and 1 cup broth. Bring to a boil; boil, stirring occasionally, until liquid has evaporated. Add SPAM® and remaining ¾ cup broth. Bring to a boil. Add parsley. In small bowl, beat together egg whites and egg. Cook vermicelli according to package directions. Drain well. Add hot pasta to SPAM™ mixture. Pour egg mixture over pasta and immediately begin lifting with 2 forks to mix well. Add 1 cup cheese. Mix until all broth is absorbed. Sprinkle top with remaining cheese.

Makes 6 servings

NUTRITIONAL INFORMATION PER SERVING:
Calories 550; Protein 34 g; Carbohydrates 61 g; Fat 18 g; Cholesterol 100 mg; Sodium 1299 mg

SPAM™ Jambalaya

SPAM™ Vegetable Strudel

1 (6-ounce) package long-grain and wild rice mix
½ cup chopped carrots
½ cup chopped red bell pepper
¼ cup orange juice
1 (12-ounce) can SPAM® Lite Luncheon Meat, cut into thin strips
2 cups chopped fresh mushrooms
¼ cup sliced green onions
1 tablespoon Dijon mustard
½ teaspoon dried basil leaves
¼ teaspoon black pepper
6 sheets frozen phyllo pastry, thawed Butter-flavored nonstick cooking spray
1 tablespoon dry bread crumbs HOUSE OF TSANG® Soy Sauce

Heat oven to 375°F. Prepare rice according to package directions. In small saucepan, combine carrots, bell pepper and orange juice. Bring to a boil. Cover and cook 5 to 7 minutes or until vegetables are crisp-tender. Drain well. Transfer vegetable mixture to medium bowl.

In large skillet, sauté SPAM®, mushrooms and green onions until tender. Add SPAM™ mixture, rice, mustard, basil and black pepper to vegetable mixture; stir well.

Place 1 sheet phyllo pastry on damp towel (keep remaining phyllo covered). Lightly coat phyllo pastry with cooking spray. Layer remaining 5 sheets phyllo pastry on first sheet, lightly coating each sheet with cooking spray. Spoon SPAM™ mixture onto phyllo stack, leaving a ½-inch border. Roll phyllo jelly-roll style, starting with long side containing SPAM™ mixture. Tuck ends under; place diagonally, seam side down, on baking sheet coated with cooking spray. Lightly coat top of pastry with cooking spray and sprinkle with bread crumbs. Make 12 (¼-inch-deep) diagonal slits across top of pastry using sharp knife. Bake 20 minutes or until golden. Serve with soy sauce.

Makes 6 servings

NUTRITIONAL INFORMATION PER SERVING:
Calories 265; Protein 14 g; Carbohydrates 34g; Fat 8 g; Cholesterol 45 mg; Sodium 1093 mg

SPAM™ Meal in One

¼ cup packed brown sugar
¼ cup stone-ground mustard
¼ cup beer
½ teaspoon celery seed
8 new potatoes, cut into ¼-inch-thick slices
2 cups ¼-inch-thick carrot slices
1 onion, thinly sliced
1 (12-ounce) can SPAM® Lite Luncheon Meat, sliced

Heat oven to 375°F. In small bowl, combine brown sugar, mustard, beer and celery seed. Divide vegetables and SPAM® among four 12-inch squares of foil. Drizzle mustard mixture over vegetables. Fold foil to form packets. Bake 45 to 60 minutes or until hot.

Makes 4 servings

NUTRITIONAL INFORMATION PER SERVING:
Calories 411; Protein 20 g; Carbohydrates 55g; Fat 13 g; Cholesterol 68 mg; Sodium 1073 mg

Index